HEAVEN!
...BORING?

HEAVEN!
...BORING?

GREG THOMAS

ARPress
ILLUMINATING IDEAS
EMPOWERING VOICES

ARPress
45 Dan Road Suite 5
Canton, MA 02021

Hotline: 1(888) 821-0229
Fax: 1(508) 545-7580

Ordering Information:
Quantity sales. Special discounts are available on quantity purchases by corporations, associations, and others. For details, contact the publisher at the address above.

Printed in the United States of America.

ISBN-13:   Softcover   979-8-89330-975-1
             eBook   979-8-89330-976-8

Library of Congress Control Number: 2024902470

CONTENTS

FOREWORD

For the sake of full disclosure, it should be noted that, as the author's son, I am not an unbiased reviewer of this book. Besides being related to the author, I was also recruited as one of the book's editors, critics, and sounding boards. However, that does not mean that I am an automatic rubberstamp of approval; if anything, I think that as a son who is already well familiar with his father's tendency towards excessive self-deprecation, corny puns, and bombastic over-generalizations (all of which, unfortunately, he also passed down to me), I was probably a harsher critic than most.

That does not change the fact that this is a remarkable book. Departing from the beaten track of typical explorations of heaven, eternity, and the afterlife, this book explores the prospect of eternity from many different perspectives, incorporating history, biology, cosmology, and philosophy to do so. It aims at the inquisitive and eclectic amateur rather than the scholar, and combines more than 180 endnotes, annotations, and numerous additional in-text citations, together with a whimsical tone designed to entertain as well as inform and inspire critical thought.

The book begins with an explication of the central question and reasons for exploring it, before moving into the more specific avenues of inquiry pursued in subsequent chapters. Chapter 2, "Historical Perspectives on Heaven," gives insights into viewpoints of differing religions and cultures on heaven. The next two chapters, "Time" and "Cosmology," explore in layman's terms several discoveries from the past century about the fundamental nature of the universe, examining why they make many previous conceptions of the afterlife not only implausible but also unpalatable. Moving from cosmology to the realm of biology and our own physical experience, the next two chapters, "Sex" and "Special Abilities and Sensational Senses," look at how eternity might change our perspective on our present experiences and how these experiences offer hints of eternity. The final three chapters turn to the theological implications of these scientific, historical, and philosophical explorations. "Discovering the Universal Truths" offers a perspective on the general theological conclusions from a vantage point that is both unashamedly Christian and scientific. "Making Light of God" illustrates more specifically how the biblical motif of light for God's character is in fact even more helpful "in light" of the contemporary scientific understanding of what light is and how it works. Finally, "Relationship and the Search for Significance" draws the entire work to its conclusion and discusses what will be necessary to make the idea of heaven even bearable, much less desirable, on an eternal timeframe. The numerous endnotes, an Epilogue, and two appendices offer additional thoughts on subjects raised in the text.

Although it is a work that it is designed to inform, *Heaven! … Boring?* is first and foremost a labor of love. To compose it, Dad devoted whatever "spare" time he could find in the past four plus years to writing, research, editing, typing, retyping, mumbling angry words at computers, and "blood, sweat, and tears." Why? I asked him that question several times throughout this whole process. He answered, "If just one person reads this and finds it helpful, the whole thing was worth it." I can say as a matter of personal testimony that at least one person has indeed found this book helpful.

I hope that you will be another.

MICHAEL THOMAS, MA APPLIED THEOLOGY

PREFACE

"Set your minds on things above, not on
earthly things."
COLOSSIANS 3:2

Somewhere over the rainbow, way up high,
There's a land that I heard of, once in a lullaby.[1]

I have been thinking about heaven, at least intermittently, for
a long time. I remember once sitting with my older brother
and one of his friends when I was about eight years old. One
of us said, "What do you think heaven is going to be like?" There
ensued a discussion of clouds, angels, harps, and other related
topics. Before long, we concluded that it must be, "a pretty
boring place."

In the past several years, perhaps secondary to some
circumstances that have led me to face my own mortality, I
have found myself giving the topic greater contemplation—
in particular, the concept of eternity as it relates to eventual
boredom. I abhor boredom and have been blessed with an
occupation, a wife, and enough kids to seldom face that specter.
But the next life, that is a different kettle of fish. Most of us have
heard that there are no lawyers in heaven. Well, no surprise there.

It is also no surprise that there are no doctors, no police, and no undertakers. Those occupations will be forever obsolete. So how am I to avoid eternal tedium?

Why do I include topics on astronomy/astrophysics, references to math, biology, and history along with the theological considerations? I am not a theologian by training. I also am not an astrophysicist or a professional writer. One of the key notions, if not the central concept of heaven, is God. While we cannot directly observe Him from our current vantage point, I think that studying the nature of the universe, and how it functions, can give us a glimpse of some of the attributes of its Creator. In my having done so, I am awed by the complexity and pageantry of this stage on which we act out our existence.

Consequently, I am even more awed by its Creator. I'm sure several people will tell you that I'm just plain odd. Beyond that, I am just a family doctor. Or as I often refer to myself, a Body Mechanic. I guess that makes me, Gregory M. Thomas, MD, and BM. I am aware of my lack of any official qualification to write a treatise on heaven. As I was contemplating that fact, a story from Scripture came to mind about how God can use the least of us to accomplish His will. So, I originally subtitled my book, "Balaam's Donkey Is at It Again" (see Numbers 22:28). If God could use a jackass to impart wisdom once, I thought, perhaps it will please Him to do so again.

My wife and her friend concluded that the subtitle was misleading. She pointed out that the book was not supposed to be about me (I get a lot of positive strokes around here!), but about heaven. Thus, for the 99.5 percent of you who are not astrophysicists, theologians, or professional writers but are curious about the existence of God, and heaven, and eternity, what follows is my sincerest effort to convey a few insights that I think He has given me to consider, and hopefully share with others. Balaam's donkey spoke a simple truth; I hope to do the same.

GREGORY M. THOMAS, MD, BM, AND
HOPEFULLY, BD (BALAAM'S DONKEY)

John 17:3

CHAPTER 1

ETERNITY

"Show me, LORD, my life's end
And the number of my days;
Let me know how fleeting my life is.
You have made my days a mere handbreadth.
The span of my years is as nothing before you.
Everyone is but a breath."
PSALM 39:4–5

*For God so loved the world that he gave his one and only Son,
that whoever believes in him shall not perish but have eternal life.*
JOHN 3:16

Eternity is very long, especially towards the end.
WOODY ALLEN

As if you could kill time without injuring eternity.
HENRY DAVID THOREAU

Have you ever spent time considering the implications of the term eternal life? It sounds great right off the top, but when contemplated, it holds a potential major pitfall: boredom. Eternity is a long, long time.

I have occasionally spent what seemed like an eternity in various endeavors. The earliest experience I recall is first grade. I well remember standing by the radiator in Sister Bernice Marie's room, staring out the window at the world beyond and thinking about being someplace else, especially home.

Home had all that I desired, all that I needed, and all that I loved. But time had seemed to stop, and I was sure that there would be no resumption of those days of freedom, sunshine, Mom's cookies, and just being at my house.

My freshman year at Oregon State and the first year of medical school were similar, albeit tempered by the knowledge of my experience and a mind endowed with a more concrete grasp of spacetime and reality in general.

It is interesting that my next older brother conveyed a similar sentiment stated in a different way. He noted that, beginning with the first Sunday evening following his first week in first grade, he had a knot develop in the pit of his stomach. He continued to experience that same knot every Sunday evening, week after week, month after month, year after year. He felt that it would never end. Yet he finally did find sanctuary. "You know," he said, "ever since I retired, I don't get that knot anymore." I believe that this is a faint aroma of what we will experience on leaving this life and beginning the next.

There have been other occasions when I wished that I could stop time, forever lingering in the contentment in which I was enraptured. My nascent recollection of having this inclination was when I was probably about three years old, walking into the kitchen very early one summer morning. No one else was up, and the sun was just breaking through the bamboo blinds on the east side of the room. Everything was bathed in a golden light, there was absolute quiet, and I felt totally at peace, not even contemplating the day to come.

Another instance was when I brought my oldest son and daughter up to some land outside of town where our new house was under construction. The structure, in the middle of a Christmas tree farm, was being framed. It was evening and Comet Hyakutake was in the western heavens. As we were outside of town, the light of the city was distant, and there was no sound except for that of the gentle breeze. I laid on a piece of four-by-eight-foot plywood I had placed on the ground and snuggled my ten-year-old son under one arm and my eight-year-old daughter beneath the other.

The sky was soon dark except for a myriad of stars and a beautiful comet's tail pointing to this divine spectacle from God. I knew my children were sharing with me in this reverie.

Finally, I remember, a few years later, lying in bed one evening, having just turned out the light. The faint but soothing sounds of "Lights Out," a Portland, Oregon, radio station's late-night offering of various artists' works, were hovering in the room. I was struck with a profound sense of peace as I contemplated my wife asleep in my embrace and my children nestled in their beds healthy, happy, and safe. Could I have stopped time at that point, I would not be writing this sentence now.

But had I been able to pull off this aberration of nature, it would not have been fair to my loved ones, who still had so much life to know. No, it would have been totally selfish. Even that aspect aside, would I truly have found it rewarding or even tolerable? As I noted above, eternity takes in time beyond comprehension.

Having experienced seventy years of the various diversions that life offers, I have learned that, while they are excellent in the moment, tedium is seldom far behind. I remember seeing the ocean for the first time when I was about ten years old. It was overwhelming. My eyes could not drink in, nor my mind grasp, the vastness of that body of water and the sound of waves, a sound that may have been continuous for as much as the past four billion years. However, I confess that many times since then, I have visited the Pacific Ocean and, while I still feel very much at peace there and appreciative of its beauty and majesty, I no longer feel that same sense of awe.

What possible mechanisms might help provide rescue from our tendency to eventually derive banality from the extraordinary? If Satan were in charge, he might arrange for all to have Alzheimer's disease and simply not remember from one moment to the next, only cognizant of present misery. Thankfully, he will have absolutely nothing to say about what will go on in God's heavenly kingdom.

Some might argue that heaven is an entirely different type of existence, where we exist outside of a spacetime continuum. One might be able to make a cogent argument for this scenario by citing 2 Peter 3:8: "With the Lord a day is like a thousand years, and a thousand years are like a day." I develop this line of thought in Chapter 3, "Time." Simply put, in heaven there is not a before or after, a past or future, but simply existence.

The author Kurt Vonnegut[1] used this device in what is probably his best-known work, *Slaughterhouse-Five.*[2] In his novel, which entails some of his actual experiences as a prisoner of war in World War II, the protagonist, Billy Pilgrim, is a person who becomes "unstuck in time." While he himself is not omnipresent in time, his consciousness randomly journeys both forward and backward, and he encounters alien beings called Tralflamadorians, who exist in this perpetual state. Their experience is that what always was and always will be, always is, and is immutable. Their mantra is "so it goes."

As I am human and not Tralflamadorian, I find this is beyond my ability to fully comprehend in an experiential way. Knowing that in the chronological and spatial omnipresent state God still governs and interacts with our universe in a very personal way, I take the stance that heaven will not consist of this static condition but instead of an ongoing process, time without end.

Where is heaven? We can currently observe at distances of over thirteen billion light-years. But no matter which direction we look, there is no sign of heaven. Yet, as inferred from Philippians 1:23 ("I desire to depart and be with Christ") and Ephesians 1:20 ("he raised Christ from the dead and seated him at his right hand in the heavenly realms"), heaven is as near as our final earthly breath.

Second Corinthians 5:2–4 says, "Meanwhile we groan, longing to be clothed instead with our heavenly dwelling...so that what is mortal may be swallowed up by life." While I have no hope of truly revealing the implications of this profound statement, I think that it is fun to consider some of the factors that might come into play. In the following pages, I hope to stimulate your thought, build on your hope, edify your faith, and increase your anticipation of the wondrous future that God wants to give to you. If all works optimally, we will come to a more intuitive and experiential way to know God, a way much deeper than simple intellectual assent.

CHAPTER 2

HISTORICAL PERSPECTIVES ON HEAVEN

"What no eye has seen, what no ear has heard,
and what no human mind has
conceived-
the things God has prepared for those
who love him."
1 CORINTHIANS 2:9

When I die, I hope to go to Heaven,
whatever the Hell that is.
AYN RAND1

If I am not allowed to laugh in heaven,
I don't want to go there.
MARTIN LUTHER

L ike many people in my town, I like to go on the local Tour of Homes, where I essentially get the opportunity to walk through and examine new houses built by different architects and builders. I like to look at the general layout and flow of the house. I examine the functionality and décor, the vaulted ceilings, the tray lighting, the built-in stereo system, and yard features.

However, if I find a builder whose product I really like, I sometimes ask him if he has another house under construction in the area. If he does, then I inquire as to its location and ask permission to give myself an unguided tour there.

Why would I do such a thing? Perhaps it comes from watching my dad build the house in which I principally grew up. He did virtually all of it himself, and just as he did on everything else, he did his best to accomplish an outstanding product. He succeeded.

He was not a builder by training; he was a professional forester. But he was also a Renaissance man who could accomplish about anything he set his mind to and do it well—even if it did take about fifteen years to finish!

In my time in that house, I witnessed the importance of starting on a firm foundation and building at least to code or better when possible. While most people may like the look of a painting hanging on the wall, I want to know what is under the plasterboard. Consequently, I want to see how the concrete is poured, what materials they use for the studs, what type of insulation they incorporate, and how the drainage is set up.

I imagine most people would find this boring, and that brings me to this chapter, which asks this question: Is there anything in the traditional views of heaven to make me think that I can avoid boredom when I get there? While the chapter will probably lack some of the "fun" I hope to incorporate into later sections, I think it best to examine the foundation that has been laid down and see where it is solid, where it has potential faults to reckon with, and how we might best build concepts on it with which to anchor our thought.

For those of us who were raised in Western culture, it may be surprising that not everyone in the world has the same concept of heaven—or any concept of heaven, for that matter. Of course, the most telling factor in shaping our ideas about an afterlife is our concept of who or what God is.

The spectrum of beliefs spans all the way from having a belief in a very personal God who cares about us enough to number the very hairs on our head, to no form of God whatsoever. But in attempting to classify beliefs, it is important to realize that within any one religious system there is some disparity as to what might constitute an afterlife. Thus, the forthcoming statements are to be taken in general and not always specific.

Let us start at one end of the spectrum with atheism. As anyone with any concept of word origins would note, *theos* in Greek refers to God, and *a* means without. The difficulty in defining who would be in this group would be to try to sort out who is truly an atheist versus who would classify themselves as agnostic, secular, or nonreligious.

Depending on how strict one is with the definitions, it is estimated that there are between 750 million and 1.1 billion people in the world who would classify themselves within this framework. [2] I suspect that, if humanity was facing a potential extinction event, and a giant foxhole big enough to contain this atheistic sector was constructed, the numbers would be expected to drop dramatically. Some may think that discounting the possibility of God is a recent trend in human thought, but it has been around at least the past 2,500 years. "Philosophical atheist thought appears in Europe and Asia from the sixth or fifth century BCE."[3]

Today we have what are termed secular humanism and communism to carry forth the banner of non-hope. It seems to me that the adult beverage companies target their advertising at a lot of people in this camp. These advertisers seem intent on reminding consumers of their mortality, and that they only get one life in which to consume as much beer as possible.

As Paul said in 1 Corinthians 15:29–32: "Now if there is no resurrection... 'let us eat and drink, for tomorrow we die.'" This may seem bleak, but in my contemplation of what constitutes an afterlife, especially an eternal one, if heaven is not at least what I conclude it to be, then eternal existence will turn out to be ultimately intolerable. Nonexistence might be my second choice.

Next let us look at those who have a belief system that falls under the category of monism, of which there are about 1.76 billion adherents on earth.

[4] Merriam-Webster's first definition for this is "a view that there is only one kind of ultimate substance." This sounds similar, but not identical to something physicists call the Theory of Everything, [5] which I will discuss in Chapter 7, "Discovering the Universal Truths."

Where the Theory of Everything is an endeavor to discover how the entire universe could have derived from one form of energy and how it operates, and does not have any implicit theological constructs, monism holds that there is no separate supreme god in the sense that a monotheist would. Instead— and perhaps this is oversimplified— "we are all one with the universe." As with atheism, this is not a strictly recent concept of the New Age movement. Buddhism, which dates from Buddha (563–483 BC), and Hinduism, which may date back as far as 1500 BC, could both fall into this category.[6, 7, 8]

Hinduism was originally polytheistic in nature.[9] It was very much a ritualistic religion. As these rituals became more complex with time, they were eventually codified in what are known as the *Vedas*.[10] Additionally, the complexity led to a class of priests. People being what they are, the priestly class eventually became the sole mediators of how the general populace could approach the gods. This eventuated a revolt, and the "form of Hinduism that emerged after the revolt emphasized the importance of internal meditation as opposed to the external rituals. Between 800 to 300 B.C., the *Upanishads* were written…The *Upanishads* expound the idea that behind many gods stands one Reality, which is called *Brahman*. *Brahman* is an impersonal, monistic ('all is one') force. The highest form…is called *nirguna*, which means 'without attributes or qualities.'"[11] This was later modified to *saguna Brahman*, which means Brahman "with attributes."[12]

As opposed to the Hindu version of God, the Buddhist version is a little tricky for me to grasp. I find that it seems to be described in negatives.

"There is a sphere which is neither earth, nor water, nor fire, nor air, which is not the sphere of the infinity or space, nor the sphere of the infinity of consciousness, the sphere of nothingness, the sphere of perception, or non-perception."[13]

The fact that Siddhartha Gautama (563–483 B.C.), the first Buddha,[14] founded this religion as a means of escaping all human suffering[15] may explain this negative reference plane. We currently call the taking away of physical pain *analgesia*. Remember to give thanks for this next time that you visit your dentist. In the case of Buddhism, the suffering referred to is not just physical but also emotional and spiritual.

Both seem to involve birth, death, and reincarnation in a cycle of indeterminate length. In the case of Buddhism, it is until enlightenment is obtained. In that state of mind, the person realizes the end of their desire to exist as an individual and is thus freed from all desires, all suffering, and the cycle of birth and death.[16]

In Hinduism, one's immediate state depends on the karma that has been accrued. One's karma directly impacts not only one's current life but also one's reincarnated state. If you have lots of good karma, then perhaps in the next life you will be born into a better caste. If you have enough bad karma, then you may come back as something less than human.[17] Ultimately, if one can escape the idea that they are an individual and instead a part of Brahman, then they are free from further incarnation.[18]

I have created an analogy that I hope is correct to help me better understand the similarities and differences between the Hindu and Buddhist concepts of heaven. Imagine that we each exist as individual rocks on an infinitely sandy plain. If you look at pictures from the Mars Rover, then that may facilitate the imagery.

I think of the Brahman and Nirvana as being analogous to the aggregate sand. To become a part of either, the rock must lose its identity as an individual stone and be reduced to its component parts, which are, indeed, sand. Thus, when attaining this state, the sense of the "individual" is lost and is intermixed with the congregate body. One becomes a part of, and indistinguishable from, the whole.

In either belief system, that short time we spent as solid rock was merely the illusion that we were separate. In the case of Hinduism, this loss of self-results in the joining of a universal consciousness of which we have always been a part. This is generally conceived of as a state of contentment.[19]

If one adheres to Buddhism, then the resultant state is one of joining a universal existence that is in all respects numb to being existent. In either case, as the individual no longer exists, there is no one to apply karma to and thus no individual accountability. There, I hope I was able to successfully confuse a few people.

Polytheism may date back as far as 4200 years BC.[20] It was practiced by the Greeks (see Acts 17:16), the Romans,[21] Assyrians and Babylonians,[22] and peoples indigenous to the Middle East (see Exodus 34:15–16). Prehistoric peoples common to the Americas, sub-Saharan Africa and other realms were largely polytheistic. Tribal religions around the world are still a stronghold of this belief system.[23] Currently, there are thought to be a little more than 400 million polytheists inhabiting the earth.[24]

Generally speaking, the multitude of gods has to do with various aspects that were important to the continuation of life. There are gods of rain, reproductive fertility, harvest, youth, animals, plants, rocks, wine, beauty, the sun, and most other things that you can call to mind. In general, the idea is to try to appease the gods and at all costs to avoid making them angry.

As there is no one "polytheism" for people to subscribe to, it is not surprising that there is no consistent picture of heaven to which polytheists ascribe. The Egyptians believed that it would be necessary to have a body in which to be fully active in the afterlife and thus sought to assist that process through mummification. Since food and money and, in some instances, slaves were thought to be necessary for use in the next life, these were often included with the *corpus delicti* in burial.

I am confident that more than a few of the slaves would have been willing to consider an alternate belief system prior to being entombed with their late master. Life was generally considered to be a continuation of the earthly one, but "better."

The Greeks, after paying the boatman to cross the river Styx, were ultimately judged as good or bad. The bad were destined for torture and frustration. The good were destined for a lush, sun-filled paradise called the Elysian Fields.[25]

The Romans believed that, at least for the good individuals, their ultimate future was to become one of the stars in the Milky Way.[26] If one had enough wealth and political influence, then he or she might arrange to be declared a god, even prior to death.[27] Presumably, this was a "get out of jail free" card for those who "for the greater good of Rome" perpetrated some very nasty things on their fellow beings. While most polytheistic views of heaven are idealized visions of earth, some peoples also believe in reincarnation.

There seems to be principally one example of competing dualism and that is termed Zoroastrianism.[28], [29] Figures for quantity of followers vary all the way from 200,000 to 2.6 million believers.[30], [31]

This belief system arose around six centuries prior to the birth of Christ. It centers around the writings of a Persian named Zarathustra, who, as a young adult is said to have received some revelation from the creator of all that is good. This deity's name is Ahura Mazda.

Some of you may be passingly familiar with the name Zarathustra, especially if you were born in the early 1950s and happened to play in a high school band. In 1896, Richard Strauss, inspired by Nietzsche's[32] book *Also Sprach Zarathustra*, composed a symphonic poem of the same name. This composition was used as the theme song in the 1968 film *2001: A Space Odyssey.*

Ahura Mazda has an archenemy who is also very mighty, albeit ultimately not as powerful. That entity's name is Aura Mainyu, and he is the source of all that is evil. As with Christianity, man is given free choice and can join either side of the battle.

Of course, which being you pledge your allegiance to ultimately decides your eternal fate. Your choice dictates how much good and how much evil you accrue during your lifetime. After death, all deeds are placed on a scale. If the scale tilts to the good, then heaven is assured. If it tilts the other way, then hell awaits. There are ways of expunging some of the bad works by doing meritorious deeds or at least confessing to the misdeeds. Heaven is described as a place of light, purity, exultation, fragrance, comfort, pleasure, and freedom from pain, want, or distress.[33, 34, 35]

As opposed to competing dualism, balancing dualism has two equal but opposite forces of creation opposing each other, resulting in a balance of good and evil, light, and dark, which are more generally gathered under the terms of *yin* and *yang*. This equipoise, if left undisturbed, is viewed as being perfection. Hence, proponents have a view in which the goal of life is to try to live in harmony with both aspects while letting the Tao (an impersonal force of nature) flow through them.

Once again, a brief analogy may help. Imagine the Tao (pronounced "dow") as the water flowing down a brook. You could be a small boat trying to navigate the stream as you see fit. But ideally you will act as a small leaf floating on the surface, letting the stream carry you along. A turn in the streambed to the left is the yin and a turn in the streambed to the right is the yang.

Taoism (Daoism) is the primary example of this practice and there are many different schools under this general banner. There are approximately 394 million people who are thought to practice this system.[36] It dates to at least the fourth century BC in China[37] and may have formed as a reaction to Confucianism.[38]

In time, it became intermixed with Buddhism and Confucianism and does not seem to have a consistent uniform concept of the afterlife.[39, 40] The current concepts seem to have been most influenced by Buddhism.

In the purest sense, Taoism was more focused on gaining perfection in this life rather than attaining it in some future postmortem realm. It was thought that it might be possible to escape death and continue life in a perfected form that would also grant special powers. If there was a heavenlike aspect as far as a physical place then it was thought to exist somewhere on earth, somewhere unattainable and indeed invisible to the imperfect.[41] In this rarefied environment, the perfected people would be free to interact in perfect society.

If we investigate the last general schema I will discuss here, we will find three principal examples: Judaism (14 million people), Islam (1.5 billion people) and Christianity (2.1 billion people).[42] They can all be described by the term *monotheism* (one God).

Monotheists believe that there is only one God (with a big G) who transcends all the universe and is the source of creation. Just as importantly, this one God, as opposed to the monistic concept discussed above, has characteristics that make Him a distinct being: extrinsic to His creation as opposed to subject to or part of it, auto endowed with self-awareness, possessing a voice, having the ability to judge what is good and not good, enabled with a will, embodying discernment about what is sacred, capacitated with the ability to decide authority, owning the copyright on structure and function of genetic code, and manifesting the power that whatever He decrees will come to pass.

All of that and more, and that is only in the first eight verses of Genesis, which the three monotheistic religions hold as sacred and inspired. While all three groups believe in the concepts of heaven and hell and that physical death is not the end of human existence, there is great diversity as to what those constructs might entail.

Of the three, the religion with the least developed dogma about heaven is Judaism. Jewish views of the afterlife have been diversified for several millennia, and there are opinions based on interpretations of both the Torah (the five books of Moses, constituting the Pentateuch) and the Talmud (a body of writing of Jewish tradition comprising the *Mishnah* and *Gemara)*.

In Jesus' day, one of the main schisms as to the nature of the afterlife occurred between the Sadducees, who did not believe in the physical resurrection of the dead (that is why they are sad, you see), and the Pharisees, who did hold such a belief. Paul used this dichotomy of belief to extricate himself from a dicey situation when he appeared before the Sanhedrin and declared, "'My brothers, I am a Pharisee, descended from Pharisees. I stand on trial because of the hope in the resurrection of the dead.' When he said this, a dispute broke out between the Pharisees and the Sadducees, and the assembly was divided" (Acts 23:6–7).

There is apparently some debate as to what the Sadducees did believe happened in death. According to the Jewish Virtual

Library, the Sadducees "rejected the idea of the Oral Law and insisted on the literal interpretation of the Written Law; consequently, they did not believe in an afterlife since it is not mentioned in the Torah."[43]

The schism may have had to do with what goes on in the "afterlife," as both groups seemed to agree that when a person died, the soul went to Sheol, a bleak and ethereal residence for departed spirits.

Was Sheol a place of total annihilation, or a site from which one potentially could be rescued by the Lord? Jesus challenged the Sadducees' lack of belief in an afterlife in Matthew 22:32 when He quoted from Exodus 3:6: "'I am the God of Abraham, the God of Isaac, and the God of Jacob.' He is not the God of the dead but of the living."

The Pharisees were united in the existence of what is referred to in Hebrew as *Olam Ha-Ba* (the World to Come).[44] This term is used to refer to the messianic age and refers to a state in which the soul has been purified.

The Pharisees taught that the place the righteous soul will inhabit is *Gan Eden* (the Garden of Eden).[45] It is a realm of peace, bliss, and satisfaction. Some writings suggest it is a place of golden tables and utensils, banquets, and sexual intercourse; while others portray no drinking, eating, or material substance with only the souls present, and they having attained a true realization of God.[46] There is almost universal agreement that, be it in Sheol if one is a Sadducee or Gan Eden if a Pharisee, after death there was some place of gathering together with one's ancestors (see Genesis 25:17; 49:33; and others).

Of all the major religions, Islamic sacred writings seem to contain the most voluminous number of descriptive verses about heaven. In the Quranic text, this place is referred to by the term *Jannah* (paradise). [47] There are several basic tenets.

It is said to be a place that is eternal and there is great beauty and great wealth. "For them (recipients of the blessing) will be Gardens of eternity: beneath them rivers will flow; they will be adorned therein with bracelets of gold, and they will wear green garments of fine silk and heavy brocade. They will recline therein on raised thrones" (Quran, Surah Al Kahf, Chapter 18, verse 31). This is described as a place of lush vegetation where "rivers of water the taste and smell of which are not changed, rivers of milk of which the taste never changes, rivers of wine delicious to those who drink, and rivers of clarified honey" (Quran, Muhammad 47:15).

It is a place where one forever exists in the prime of life, free of disease, infirmity, or the threat of death. The righteous will be able to enjoy wine from those rivers (alcohol is prohibited by the Quran) without having it produce any intoxicating effect. [48] We are also informed that it cannot be fully comprehended in this life: "Never mind what Allah has told you; what He has not told you is even greater" (Saheeh Muslim).

Admission criteria may seem simultaneously inclusive and exclusive, depending on one's worldview. While this place is reserved for those who have worshiped only Allah, the followers of past prophets such as Abraham, Moses, and Jesus, about whom it is implied worshiped "the only true God", Allah, would also gain admittance. [49]

That statement deserves a little explanation. Islamic teaching is that there were many times when God chose to reveal Himself through inspired writing. Counted among these authors (prophets of God) were Abraham, Moses, David, Jesus, Muhammad, and more than one hundred thousand others.[50] However, while the previous writings were held as having been corrupted over time[51] (and in their current issue not reliable), Islamic doctrine holds that God used Muhammad as the final, definitive author.

To gain a fuller understanding of Jannah, we need to combine writing from the Quran with what are termed the *hadiths*. The Merriam-Webster dictionary defines these as, "the collective body of traditions relating to Muhammad and his companions." There seems to be at least some minor ambivalence on the number of levels or types of paradise. Some tie it to the number of verses in the Quran: "It will be said to the companion of the Qur'aan: 'Recite and rise in status as you used to recite in the world, and your position will be at the last verse you recite'" (hadith of 'Abd-Allaah ibn 'Amr).

There are other writings that place the believer in paradise at a level commensurate with his faith and works. Financially supporting the faith is a source of reward. Jihad (holy war for the sake of Allah) and, of course, martyrdom are means of improving your eternal standing. [52]

There is a hadith that states: "The martyr has seven blessings from Allah: he is forgiven from the moment his blood is first shed; he will be shown his place in Paradise; he will be spared the trial of the grave; and he will be secure on the Day of the Greatest Terror (Judgment Day); there will be placed on his head a crown of dignity, one ruby of which is better than this world and all that is in it; he will be married to seventy-two *hoor al-'ayn* (the Quran itself does not specify this number); and he will be permitted to intercede for seventy of his relatives."[53]

However, it seems that martyrdom is not a prerequisite for all great reward. Al-Tirmidhi, Vol. 4, Ch. 21, No. 2687 contains the following: "The smallest reward for people of Heaven is an abode where there are eighty thousand servants and seventy-two houri, over which stands a dome decorated with pearls, aquamarine and ruby, as wide as the distance from alJabiyyah to San'a." The highest degree of paradise is said to be al-Firdaws, which is said to be the closest in proximity to Allaah. "…When you ask Allaah, ask Him for al-Firdaws, for it is in the middle of Paradise and is the highest part of Paradise, and above it is the Throne of the Most Merciful, and from it spring forth the rivers of Paradise" (al-Bukhaari, 2637; Muslim, 2831).

While the blessings per se all seem to be well and good, not all of them are seen as equal when it comes to being a motivator, at least for men, for desiring to be numbered among the elect. Islam has what are probably the most provocative depictions of heaven (paradise). While the Quran gives many references [54] to a reward of dark-eyed virgins with fair skin and large breasts to be given as brides *(hoor al-'ayn or huris or houri),* the hadiths give much more extensive, and in some cases explicit, detail. I will try to convey the concepts, albeit in a toned-down manner.

"In classical Arabic, *Hur'in* is made of two words *Hur* and *In.* The former word literally means 'most beautiful eye' irrespective of the person's gender, while the latter word means 'companion.' Thus, the English rendering of the compound word Hur'in is 'pure companions with most beautiful eyes.'"[55] They are described as beautiful, hairless except for their head and brows, modest, companions of equal age (all young and in their prime), voluptuous and sensual, pure, ever virginal (even after intercourse with their husband).[56, 57, 58]

I have always loved the imagery and lighting in Maxfield Parrish's[59] painting *Garden of Allah,* though, as you may find, there may be reason to question if he got all the details correct. If you are a male reading this, then you may be thinking that this version of heaven sounds very inviting. Like a good infomercial, the description of the afterlife continues with a "but wait, there's more!" The males are granted attributes to help them take full advantage of the situation like eternal erections [60] and, at least from my reading of this, potency to have 100 consecutive orgasms without need for respite.[61]

However, and perhaps it is a matter of personal taste, I do find what I would consider to be some potential (no pun intended) impediments to this eternal bliss. According to the hadith of Sahih Bukhari (Vol.4, Book 54, number 476), the *houri* will be transparent so that "the marrow of the bones of their legs will be seen through the bones and the flesh." Also, each one of these *houri* are said to be 60 cubits (90 feet) tall (Sahih Bukhari: Vol 4, book 55, number 544) and 7 cubits (10 ½ feet) wide (Al Ghazzali, Ihya Uloom Ed-Din Vol. 4).[62]

Multiply that times 72 and you have got a lot of woman to keep happy. I do not find any reference to the males being changed in size, but perhaps I missed it. If they are changed in size by a commensurate amount, then does it make any difference if those involved are both 90 feet tall or both 9 feet tall or both 9 inches tall? If the male is not changed in stature, then I do not see how this is mechanically going to be very good for either party.

Also, I cannot help but think that there would be danger intrinsic to having even consensual sex with a partner who is 15 times your height and roughly 735 times your body mass. It is not difficult to imagine that in the throes of sexual ecstasy, the *houri* might unintentionally inflict grievous bodily harm on her partner.

However, let us assume for the time being that everything works well for all concerned. The recipient of the blessing let's call him Yusuf, or Kim if you prefer, [63] has a beautiful place to live, great food and drink, fine clothes (when he can find time to wear them!), and seventy-two most beautiful houri clamoring for his sexual attention. Pessimist that I am, I still see a dark cloud on the horizon.

Dolf Zillman of Indiana University prepared a paper for the Surgeon General's Workshop on Pornography and Public Health (Arlington, Virginia, June 22–24, 1986). It was titled "Effects of Prolonged Consumption of Pornography." He cites several references, including a 1971 paper by Reifler, Howard, Lipton, Liptzen and Widman, that endeavored to explore the effects of pornography consumption in male college students and later reaction to pornography.

A couple of conclusions are worth noting. "The findings show that the young men initially had a strong interest in pornographic films. However, this interest faded with repeated consumption…. What the study does show is that consumers of pornography grow tired of watching the same materials repeatedly."

Let us reconsider the case of the seventy-two virgins. In the scope of eternity, if Yu-Kim has sex with ten different houri each day, then he will start to repeat that cycle about once a week. So, in a month he will have had sex with each one about four times. In a year, he will have had sex with each one of them about fifty times. In ten years, he has had sex with each of them five hundred times, and in one hundred years, five thousand times. But eternity is a long time. In only a billion years he will have had sex with each one of them fifty billion times. Fifty billion is a large number. (For example, that many seconds would amount to about 870 years.) Now you start to see the problem. It does not matter how beautiful the houri is. Given enough exposure, even the finest meal has less appeal than week-old meatloaf.

Perhaps I am just not adventurous enough, but eternity is a very long time, and any activity in which I am supposed to be engaged over that time deserves thorough contemplation.

I realize that the above discussion has already alienated one-half of my audience, and you are not alone. According to what information I could gather on the Internet,[64] modern Islamic women have some misgivings about their reward in the afterlife. It is said that the Quran does not specifically address women's rewards, but it is also said that at least some verses in the hadiths can be taken in a gender-neutral way.[65]

Christian literature regarding heaven is much tamer by comparison, although some of the imagery is unusual to say the least. Perhaps we should start by thinking what heaven is not like.

I think that Hollywood has given us a much better sampling of what might be entailed in hell (browse through movies available on the internet) than of heaven. In the movies, heaven has traditionally been shown as a very misty place. Perhaps this was intentional with respect to our lack of comprehension of heaven or perhaps it was just less expensive to film a "heavenly" scene on some San Francisco pier.

In any case, one is likely to see few inhabitants (human or celestial) in any one scene, and where does that harp music keep coming from? As much as I enjoy Harpo Marx[66] playing (including a little jazz harp!) in the 1940 Marx Brothers movie

Go West,[67] a steady diet of harp music would be like gorging on popcorn—soon it's time for a change of menu. (If you're watching a fog-filled scene that might be heaven and there is instead a background of accordion music, expect the subject of the shot to shortly come to a very nasty realization!)

All in all, it is very "vanilla" in nature, and you might wonder why anyone would want to spend five minutes there, let alone an eternity. Unfortunately, this type of imagery is where a lot of people base their concept of the kingdom of God. Hence, they may find themselves saying things like, "Well, if that's heaven, then I think I want the other place because that's where all the fun people are." This, as I hope to show in the rest of this book, is the very antithesis of the truth.

Now I want to look at concepts that have been in place since the inception of the Christian faith.

The first descriptors we have of heaven deal with the concept of doing away with our current heavens and earth. This is not an idea unique to the New Testament but instead finds its roots in the Old Testament writings of Isaiah.

Isaiah 65:17 states, "See, I will create new heavens and a new earth. The former things will not be remembered, nor will they come to mind." He continues in chapter 66, verses 22–23: "'As the new heavens and the new earth that I make will endure before me,' declares the LORD, 'so will your name and descendants endure. From one New Moon to another and from one Sabbath to another, all mankind will come and bow down before me,' says the LORD."

Note the plural on heavens. Given the Judaic culture at the time of Isaiah's writing, I would venture to say that this is not heaven, the abode of God, per se, but rather a reference to the atmospheric heavens (see discussion of the "third heaven" below). There is reason to assume that the celestial heavens may not yet be involved as there is still mention of the passing of the months (one new moon to another) and the weeks (one Sabbath to another). In Revelation 21:1 we see continuation of the concept of our current earthly abode passing away, "Then I saw 'a new heaven and a new earth,' for the first heaven and the first earth had passed away, and there was no longer any sea."

In this scenario we next encounter what might be termed the capital city of heaven, known as the New Jerusalem. Revelation 21:2–3 says, "I saw the Holy City, the new Jerusalem, coming down out of heaven from God, prepared as a bride beautifully dressed for her husband. And I heard a loud voice from the throne saying, 'Look! God's dwelling place is now among the people, and he will dwell with them. They will be his people and God himself will be with them and be their God.'"

Later in chapter 21 there are more details about the physical structure of the city. I will list only some here. From what I can discern, the New Jerusalem is laid out in the form of a cube that is 1400 miles on each side and has walls 200 feet thick that are made of jasper. As opposed to the forever fogbound visions from Hollywood, the city itself is "gold and pure as glass," has precious stones decorating it, has foundations of jasper, sapphire, agate, emerald, onyx, ruby, chrysolite, beryl, topaz, turquoise, jacinth, and amethyst... "dazzled by the brilliancy of the wonderful City. The streets were lined with beautiful houses all built of green marble and studded everywhere with sparkling emeralds... pavement of the same green marble, and where the blocks were joined together were rows of emeralds, set closely, and glittering in the brightness of the sun."

Oops! Somehow in those last couple of sentences I slipped from a description of the New Jerusalem to a description of the Emerald City from L. Frank Baum's *The Wonderful Wizard of Oz!*[68] Okay, call me a cynic, but being raised in small town America, I just never have been one for much "glitz"—golden this, silver that, ruby those (and on it goes).

While impressive to look at, there are not many things in the description that I would really be eager to see. In fact, without those few things, were I to take a tour of the city, I might respond as one of my nephews did to another experience. My next older brother and his wife and four children were visiting, and I wanted to take them out to my favorite Szechuan restaurant. While my brother and his wife enjoyed the food, I think the kids were a little underwhelmed at not having a burger and fries. As we departed the establishment, my young nephew Jesse drew my attention. "Uncle Greg, thanks, that was great. But let's not come back here for at least a year."

So, what would I really look forward to experiencing there? Most impressively, "It shone with the glory of God" (Revelation 21:11). "The city does not need the sun or the moon to shine on it, for the glory of God gives it light, and the Lamb is its lamp" (v. 23).

Secondly, the river of the water of life flowing from the throne of God and the Lamb and the tree of life standing on each side of the river is described in Revelation 22:1–2. It sounds even prettier than a late afternoon in the summer on the Deschutes River at Mirror Pond in Bend, Oregon, where I was raised.

There are what must be a rather common sight in heaven: beings referred to as angels. Heaven is inhabited by at least 100 million faithful angels (Revelation 5:11). As to what form or forms these special creations have, I am not sure. As much as I love some of the angelic renderings of Bouguereau[69] (French 1825–1905), including "Song of Angels" (1881), "A Soul Brought to Heaven" (1878), and the somewhat whimsical "The Return of Spring" (1886), I suspect that the angelic lot are more varied than we imagine.

Revelation chapter 4 describes four living creatures with unusual combinations of features, including six wings each and enough eyes that, were cataracts possible in heaven, one creature could keep an ophthalmologist busy for weeks! We know that angels were referenced as far back as Genesis 3:24: "After he drove the man out, he placed on the east side of the Garden of Eden cherubim and a flaming sword flashing back and forth to guard the way to the tree of life."

In Numbers 22:27–28 we read about my old friend and namesake, Balaam's donkey: "When the donkey saw the angel of the LORD, it lay down under Balaam, and he was angry and beat it with his staff. Then the LORD opened the donkey's mouth, and it said to Balaam, 'What have I done to you to make you beat me these three times?'"

We know that you do not want to unnecessarily provoke an angel. In 2 Kings 19:35 we read, "That night the angel of the LORD went out and put to death a hundred and eighty-five thousand in the Assyrian camp." (That is a higher body count than most Arnold Schwarzenegger movies!)

Keeping this in mind, we would do well not to slander demons (see 2 Peter 2:10 and Jude 1:8–9) or to try and battle them under our own power, as their origin is literally angelic. "For if God did not spare angels when they sinned, but sent them to hell, putting them in chains of darkness to be held for judgment" (2 Peter 2:4).

In Acts 19:14–16 we read, "Seven sons of Sceva, a Jewish chief priest, were doing this [trying to drive out demons from the possessed in Jesus' name; it is implied that they were not actually believers themselves but using it more as an incantation]. One day the evil spirit answered them, 'Jesus I know, and Paul I know about, but who are you?' Then the man who had the evil spirit jumped on them and overpowered them all. He gave them such a beating that they ran out of the house naked and bleeding."

As to there being 100 million angels present, well, as you might have guessed, I'm not much for crowds either. While I am sure they are magnificent creatures, I am not sure how long I could spend watching them.

I have gone whale watching, and those animals are truly spectacular beasts. But a couple of hours and I'm done. This might be more like bird watching. "Look folks, coming around the far side of the steeple! Does everybody see it? Good! Now let's be quiet for a few seconds and listen. Did everybody hear that? Okay. Now you can cross the six-winged, golden-throated, thunder thrower off your list!"

Do not get me wrong. I am not demeaning angels. They are in fact spectacular beyond belief and my skepticism may once again be based on my lack of imagination. But anything that I am going to look at for eternity must eventually lose some of its intrigue to me. I hope I've not offended any angels here—that was not my intent. However, I am pretty sure that they are not feeling slighted.

Those angelic beings that have remained loyal to God know they are not to be worshiped; instead, they find their fulfillment in giving glory to God, as we should. In fact, should you encounter an angel who does demand to be worshiped, you have just met the enemy.

Principally, we know heaven to be the dwelling place of God. One of the earlier references to this is from Exodus 20:22: "Then the LORD said to Moses, 'Tell the Israelites this: "You have seen for yourselves that I have spoken to you from heaven."'"

Then in Deuteronomy 26:15 there is testimony that the Jewish people believed this to be true: "Look down from heaven, your holy dwelling place, and bless your people, Israel."

Jesus certainly subscribed to the idea as demonstrated in Matthew 6:9– 10: "This, then, is how you should pray: 'Our Father in heaven, hallowed be your name, your kingdom come, your will be done, on earth as it is in heaven.'"

Finally, we have testimony from the church fathers, as noted in Acts 7:55: "But Stephen, full of the Holy Spirit, looked up to heaven and saw the glory of God, and Jesus standing at the right hand of God."

Secondly, we know heaven to be a place of reward for those who have found their way to a saving relationship with God. In 2 Kings 2:1 we read, "When the LORD was about to take Elijah up to heaven in a whirlwind…"

One of the earliest references that we find Jesus making to this was in the Beatitudes in Matthew 5:3: "Blessed are the poor in spirit, for theirs is the kingdom of heaven." He makes more than half a dozen other references to this being the final dwelling place for what He would term his brothers and sisters (Mark 3:35) or children of God (Matthew 5:9 and 5:44–45).

The apostle Paul makes several references to heaven as a final destination. In 2 Corinthians 5:2, "Meanwhile we groan, longing to be clothed instead with our heavenly dwelling."

Albeit somewhat tangential to the direct subject, there are verses later in 2 Corinthians (12:2–4) that were always somewhat of a mystery to me: "I know a man in Christ who fourteen years ago was caught up to the third heaven… was caught up to paradise and heard inexpressible things."

For me this raised two questions: What is the "third heaven"?

What is paradise, and is it then a part of heaven?

As you have read above, Muslims (those who believe and follow Islamic teaching) believe in many degrees of heaven. Was I to believe that as a Christian I should also subscribe to this view? This concept seemed to fly in the face of all that I have come to believe about my faith and my standing before God. I think of verses like Ephesians 2:4–9:

"But because of his great love for us, God, who is rich in mercy, made us alive with Christ even when we were dead in transgressions—it is by grace you have been saved. And God raised us up with Christ and seated us with him in the heavenly realms in Christ Jesus, in order that in the coming ages he might show the incomparable riches of his grace, expressed in his kindness to us in Christ Jesus. For it is by grace you have been saved, through faith—and this is not from yourselves, it is the gift of God—not by works, so that no one can boast."

To me this has several clear implications. First, we are made alive in Christ—not some of us alive while others only sort of alive; we all shall have full life. Second, it is not by works that we attain this life but by faith; therefore, our merit before God is not based on us but on Jesus. And we are seen as seated with Jesus at the right hand of God. How many Jesuses are there? One. How many right hands does God have? One. Therefore, there can be only one destination, one level of heaven, and it is there in Christ. How is this possible? Well, now you must read the rest of this little book.

For helping me resolve this quandary of the "third heaven," I was led to the website of the Christian Apologetics and Research Ministry (http://carm.org). It provided what I found to be a most satisfactory explanation: "At the time of ancient Israel they did not have as complete an understanding of the universe as we do today.... The Jews spoke of three heavens. The first heaven consisted of the earth's atmosphere where the clouds and birds were. The second heaven was where the sun, stars, and moon were. The third heaven was the dwelling place of God." Paul, not only a Jew but also a Pharisee, would likely have had this same reference plane describing the dwelling place of God.

With respect to the nature of paradise, perhaps our best clue comes from Luke 23:42–43. The scene is Golgotha and Jesus is affixed to His cross with condemned men on either side of Him. "Then he said, 'Jesus, remember me when you come into your kingdom.' Jesus answered him, 'Truly I tell you, today you will be with me in paradise.'"

Let us then take this verse and combine it with John 20:17: "Jesus said, 'Do not hold on to me, for I have not yet ascended to the Father.'" To me this seems to imply that paradise is probably a place of consciousness, peace, beauty, life, and well-being, created by God but not yet indwelt by Him, at least at that time.

Jesus visited paradise the day He was crucified. Three days later we find that he had not yet been to the Father. I think that it would be a reasonable contention that once Jesus had ascended to the Father, the opening of the doorway to God's presence was complete and the souls of those who inhabited paradise now had direct access to the Father. This does not necessarily mean that they left paradise; it is more that they began to experience heaven.

Using very similar reasoning, N. T. Wright[70] seems to reach that same conclusion. He then goes on to point out in his work *Surprised by Hope*,[71] that the early church certainly seemed to adhere to a doctrine of a two-step process toward our final realized salvation form.

The first part is the salvation of the soul. In Matthew 11:29, Jesus said, "Take my yoke upon you and learn from me, for I am gentle and humble in heart, and you will find rest for your souls."

First Peter 1:8–9 says, "Though you have not seen him, you love him; and even though you do not see him now, you believe in him and are filled with an inexpressible and glorious joy, for you are receiving the end result of your faith, the salvation of your souls."

The Psalmist certainly believed in the concept of God's salvation of the soul. Psalm 62:5–7 says, "Yes, my soul, find rest in God; my hope comes from him. Truly he is my rock and my salvation; he is my fortress, I will not be shaken. My salvation and my honor depend on God; he is my mighty rock, my refuge." In Psalm 23:6, David expresses his belief in eternal life with God:

"Surely your goodness and love will follow me all the days of my life, and I will dwell in the house of the LORD forever."

Given this mind-set, it seems likely David saw heaven as a place of reunion with loved ones. In 2 Samuel 12 we find that Bathsheba has just given birth to David's illegitimate son and that son has just died. In verses 22–23, David told his attendants: "While the child was still alive, I fasted and wept. I thought, 'Who knows? The LORD may be gracious to me and let the child live.' But now that he is dead, why should I go on fasting? Can I bring him back again? I will go to him, but he will not return to me.'"

As to the physical resurrection of the dead, I referenced earlier the divergence of opinion between the Pharisees and Sadducees. The Christian church bases its theology about heaven on the physical resurrection of Christ. As Paul so bluntly stated it in 1 Corinthians 15:32, "If the dead are not raised, 'Let us eat and drink, for tomorrow we die.'" Following that, in verses 35–57, he gives what I find to be one of the most detailed and inspirational descriptions in scripture of what the believer has to anticipate:

"But someone will ask, "How are the dead raised? With what kind of body will they come?" How foolish! What you sow does not come to life unless it dies. When you sow, you do not plant the body that will be, but just a seed, perhaps of wheat or of something else. But God gives it a body as he has determined, and to each kind of seed he gives its own body. Not all flesh is the same: People have one kind of flesh, animals have another, birds another and fish another. There are also heavenly bodies and there are earthly bodies; but the splendor of the heavenly bodies is one kind, and the splendor of the earthly bodies is another. The sun has one kind of splendor, the moon another and the stars another; and star differs from star in splendor.

So will it be with the resurrection of the dead. The body that is sown is perishable, it is raised imperishable; it is sown in dishonor, it is raised in glory; it is sown in weakness, it is raised in power; it is sown a natural body, it is raised a spiritual body.

If there is a natural body, there is also a spiritual body. So, it is written: "The first man Adam became a living being"; the last Adam, a life-giving spirit. The spiritual did not come first, but the natural, and after that the spiritual. The first man was of the dust of the earth; the second man is of heaven. As was the earthly man, so are those who are of the earth; and as is the heavenly man, so also are those who are of heaven. And just as we have borne the image of the earthly man, so shall we bear the image of the heavenly man.

I declare to you, brothers and sisters, that flesh and blood cannot inherit the kingdom of God, nor does the perishable inherit the imperishable. Listen, I tell you a mystery: We will not all sleep, but we will all be changed—in a flash, in the twinkling of an eye, at the last trumpet. For the trumpet will sound, the dead will be raised imperishable, and we will all be changed. For the perishable must clothe itself with the imperishable, and the mortal with immortality. When the perishable has been clothed with the imperishable, and the mortal with immortality, then the saying that is written will come true:

"Death has been swallowed up in victory."

"Where, O death, is your victory? Where, O death, is your sting?"

"The sting of death is sin, and the power of sin is the law. But thanks be to God! He gives us the victory through our Lord Jesus Christ."

We can analyze these verses in the light of Matthew 24:30–31 where Jesus states, "Then will appear the sign of the Son of Man in heaven. And then all the peoples of the earth will mourn when they see the Son of Man coming on the clouds of heaven, with power and great glory. And he will send his angels with a loud trumpet call, and they will gather his elect from the four winds, from one end of the heavens to the other."

Also look at 1 Thessalonians 4:14–17: "For we believe that Jesus died and rose again, and so we believe that God will bring with Jesus those who have fallen asleep in him. According to the Lord's word, we tell you that we who are still alive, who are left until the coming of the Lord, will certainly not precede those who have fallen asleep. For the Lord himself will come down from heaven, with a loud command, with the voice of the archangel and with the trumpet call of God, and the dead in Christ will rise first. After that, we who are still alive and are left will be caught up together with them in the clouds to meet the Lord in the air. And so we will be with the Lord forever." We can conclude that the early church believed that upon death the soul is immediately ushered into the presence of Jesus, and therefore the Father, while the bodily resurrection to our final and eternal state of being takes place upon His return to the earth.[72]

When reading the above passages, I get the mental image of the resurrection of the dead as being akin to a pop-up toaster. While the physical appearance might look that way to a bystander observing the event, I believe that the actual thing experienced by those asleep in Christ will be somewhat different.

35

I do not see this as an early morning alarm clock going off or the unanticipated loud blast of reveille. I like to break the call to glory down into two parts: the message and the voice.

I think that the message will be much more similar to what we read in Song of Songs 2:10-13 than to an angelic drill sergeant or a celestial rooster.

My beloved spoke and said to me,
"Arise, my darling, my beautiful one, come with me. See!
The winter is past; the rains are over and gone.
Flowers appear on the earth; the season of singing has
come, the cooing of doves is heard in our land
The fig tree forms its early fruit; the blossoming vines spread
their fragrance.
Arise, come, my darling; my beautiful one, come with me."

As to the voice, it does not matter what language you speak. The second that you hear that sound you will know beyond any doubt what it is and to whom it belongs. This is not necessarily a matter of excessive volume. It is the distinct and unreproducible character of the *sound* that will make immediate compliance the only option. Every fiber of your being will resonate at that utterance. Our concept of the term sound is too empty to begin to describe that force so awesome in majesty and power that it spoke the universe into existence. It is the voice of the Master and no matter who you are or were, at some point you will hear it.

Finally, and most importantly to the first-century church and to us, is the knowledge that as "brothers" and "sisters" and "children of God" (as referenced above), we shall be like him: "Dear friends, now we are children of God, and what we will be has not yet been made known. But we know that when Christ appears, we shall be like him, for we shall see him as he is" (1 John 3:2).

"We shall be like him." But what does that mean and what implications does that have for avoiding tedium in eternity?

Because, for my part, the descriptions of heaven thus far have not given me substantial hope for eluding eventual boredom. Before we can hope to start to gain some grasp on escaping the trap of inevitable banality, we should first try to obtain some faint concept of time and eternity.

CHAPTER 3

TIME

"With the Lord a day is like a thousand years,
and a thousand years are like a day."
2 PETER 3:8

*Lost time is never found again. BENJAMIN
FRANKLIN*

*I must govern the clock, not be governed by it.
GOLDA MEIR*

*The present is a point just past.
DAVID RUSSELL*

Christians tend to glibly state that they are going to spend "eternity with the Lord." So, what is eternity? When I checked my phone application of the Merriam-Webster Dictionary I was somewhat surprised *not to* find among the definitions, "time without end." Of course, that merely begs a definition for the word *time*.

On looking up the word *time*, I find lots of definitions like: "the measured, or measurable period, during which an action, process, or condition exists or continues" and "a non-spatial continuum that is measured in terms of events that succeed one another from past through present to future," and so on.

Unfortunately, none of the definitions I found does an adequate job of telling me just *what* time is. Prior to considering what we think that we know about time in general, I think it behooves us to consider where God fits into that construct.

There are some, even within Christendom, who propose that God Himself is subject to the effects of time. Following the writings of Alfred North Whitehead, adherents of Process Theology believe that "Just as the entire universe is in constant flow and change, God, as source of the universe, is viewed as growing and changing."[1]

A very nice drawing by the talented and creative Dutch graphic artist M.C. Escher comes to mind as a possible way to conceptualize this viewpoint. The work is titled Drawing Hands. Many of you have probably seen this piece or something like it and have been inspired by it. What the picture shows are two hands seemingly springing from a single piece of paper. Each hand is holding a pencil and is actively engaged in creating or modifying the drawing that is the other hand.

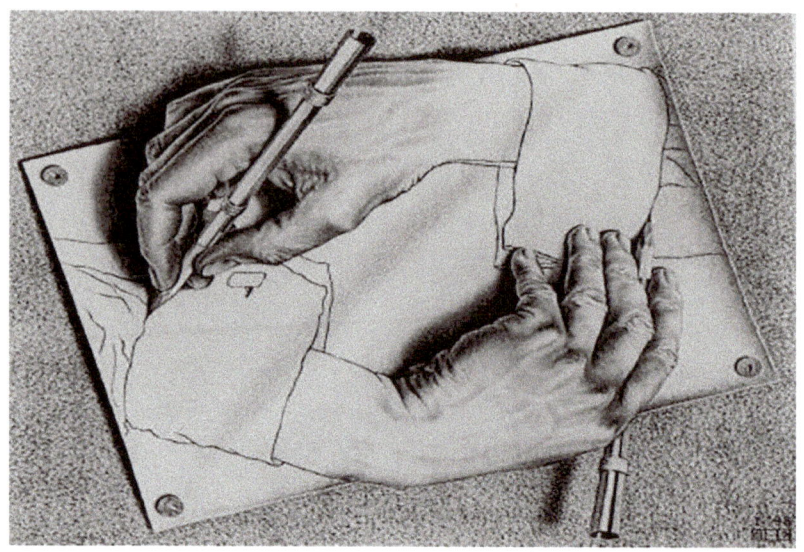

"DRAWING HANDS" BY M.C. ESCHER[2]

This is, of course, antithetical to Malachi 3:6 where we read, "I the LORD do not change," and to James 1:17, "Every good and perfect gift is from above, coming down from the Father of the heavenly lights, who does not change like shifting shadows." Also consider Hebrews 13:8: "Jesus Christ is the same yesterday and today and forever."

This supposed plasticity of God makes very little sense from a cosmological standpoint. I hope to demonstrate later in this book that creation implicitly includes the genesis of matter, space, energy, and time. Thus, for God to have created those elements, He must have existence outside of it; that is to say, He cannot be a product of it. As I study *Drawing Hands* in greater detail, I love the wit and artistic talent that went into its creation.

Yet my intellect—limited as it is—forces me to come to a simple conclusion: This picture did not create itself. To assume that this work generated itself would be absurd. Instead, it was fashioned by an unseen master. The hand of the author of the image was not really changed by the hands that were drawn.

In an analogous way, to consider God as a malleable part of the creation makes no more sense. Like Escher, God is the invisible artist. Yet, the fact that the beautiful and complex work exists is testimony to His existence.

We may be tempted to wonder what there was "before" the universe came into being. I believe that the simple but correct answer is that there was not *anything*; nor was there any before. These portions of our existence are simply tools invented by God. He is, was, and will always exist—but He is not confined to the is, was, or will be.

A moderately simple analogy may help. Consider that all of what we call space, matter, and energy are transformed into a digital video disc (DVD). In that case, *time* will act as the DVD player and what is witnessed on the video screen is our current reality. While each of us shows up at some point on that display, we are not to be seen there constantly. Indeed, we are not there, then we are, and finally we are not there again, not to be seen again for the rest of the movie.

There is someone watching that video. He is the one who conceived of the movie in the first place, made it, and placed it on the DVD. However, this is a special edition 3-D, Blu-ray DVD that has an added feature to it. The viewer/creator has the capability to interact with the characters at any place in the movie when he deems it appropriate. Because he is not confined to the DVD and controls the player also, he can skip backward to the beginning, skip ahead to the end, fast motion, slow motion, reverse motion, or watch along.

Like some people I know, he has this movie memorized and can quote all of the lines, knows how long each scene lasts, and can list every major and minor person who appears in the movie. I know that you have surmised who it is viewing this feature. Some people in the movie have guessed that they are being watched and have become curious about the viewer. They want to know how old he is. They have not considered that "old" only applies to how far along something is into the recording on the DVD.

As he is not confined to that media, as the Creator is not bound to the creation, he has no age. He simply exists and exists in a way that is far more profound than anything anyone in the movie can conceive of. He is true. He is real. And they are, at best, simply two or three-dimensional images. There have been a few occasions on which he has tried to share this perspective with them by saying something like, "I am the Alpha and the Omega, the First and the Last, the Beginning and the End" (Revelation 22:13), and even more concisely, "I AM" (Exodus 3:14). The characters are a little slow on the uptake.

I think this has very real implications with respect to the state in which we will spend our eternity and therefore how it impacts our ability to be bored. As I see it, when we die and go to heaven, it could either consist of a place where there is no time, a place where there is time but no aging, or a place where things like dimensions and time have no meaning. That is what I will call *the God place*, for lack of a better term. It is that realm occupied only by God.

I would argue against there being a place with no time because, at least as I understand existence, it would be very difficult to have any interaction with anyone or anything in that case. For reasons I hope to illuminate later, I think that we are created specifically for interaction and therefore discount the premise of the stagnant state.

I do not believe heaven to consist of the God place either. While this would perhaps allow for interaction—and I do think that we will be able to interact with that realm—to be in that realm, we would literally have to become God. While there have been lots of people in asylums (and a few in political offices!) who have thought that they were God, they were proven to be sadly mistaken. No, the Creator is the Creator, and the creation is the creation.

That leaves the other scenario in which there is a literal place where we are capable of living forever, interacting with God and fellow inhabitants. For reasons that I will bring out in the discussion about cosmology (that branch of astronomy dealing with the origin and structure of the universe and its relationships to space and time) we are going to need a fundamentally different universe in which to spend that time.

What do we know about time itself? St. Augustine[3] (AD 354–430) in his writing *Confessions* summed up what is still a viable synopsis of what we understand to be the nature of time:

"What then is time? Is there any short and easy answer to that? Who can put the answer into words or even see it in his mind? Yet what commoner or more familiar word do we use in speech than time? Obviously when we use it, we know what we mean, just as when we hear another use it, we know what he means. What then is time? If no one asks me, I know; if I want to explain it to a questioner, I do not know."

Time is not what you think it is; but, on the other hand, it is exactly what you think it is. The first dichotomy I consider in tackling this subject is the difference between time the *substance* and time the *subjective*. We tend to accept the thing as an immutable truth of our daily existence: There are 60 seconds in a minute, 60 minutes in an hour, 24 hours in a day, and so on. By contrast, our subjective perception of time is our personal experience of its passage. This by its nature is less orderly and varies from person to person and event to event. I will discuss subjective time first.

Have you ever been in a situation in which time expanded and seemed to slow down? I do not refer to the colloquial "I had a long day" type experience, but one in which there seemed to be a slowing of the passage of an event.

I recall several experiences from my youth when I was witnessing something as if it were happening in slow motion. On one occasion I was riding along on the back of another kid's bike. (Remember those balloon-tired bikes that were one speed and had carrying racks on the back?) I was seated securely; that is, until he hit a pothole in the dirt road. I recall being lifted from my perch by the impact. My legs and body subsequently slowly unfurled behind me like a flag on a windy day while I clung to the back of the bike seat with my hands.

As I lost my grip, I remember noting that my posture was somewhat like that of one of my favorite fictional characters of the time, Superman in full flight. I watched the ground approach me as one might experience the nearing of a runway from an airplane window seat. Thankfully, this landing strip, not being asphalt, was much more forgiving. Thus, my landing was less catastrophic than it might have otherwise been.

I venture to say that virtually all of us have experienced compressed time. Our heads may just seem to hit the pillow when the alarm "instantly" sounds to start another day.

Sometimes this phenomenon works to our advantage. I have had the experience of being fully awake while undergoing a rigid sigmoidoscopy. A rigid sigmoidoscope is a pipe about fifteen inches long and about three quarters of an inch in diameter. However (maybe I should make that "Owever"!), it felt fully three times that length and diameter when I was the object of its use.

As you might derive from the name, it is used to view the sigmoid colon. The sigmoid portion of the colon was named thus by our Greek predecessors because of its S shape. It does not take a lot of imagination to see the inherent difficulty of reconciling a sigmoid shape to a linear one.

I have also experienced a colonoscopy, done with a colonoscope about seven feet long and one-half inch in diameter but fully flexible and, at least in my case, administered while I was under the influence of a drug called Versed. This remarkable chemical not only induces a sleep-like state but also has the added benefit of some degree of retrograde amnesia. In other words, not only are you likely not to hurt, but you are even less likely to remember it if you did! Given my choice of the two experiences, I much prefer the compressed time experience, though I still don't fully understand how I ended up sitting in that chair with my clothes back on.

Unfortunately, compressed time has also landed me in some trouble with a few select people. I want to make it a matter of public record that Pastor Al Perkins preaches great sermons. They are well researched, thorough, and very interesting. Is it my fault that he made me feel so secure and at peace in church that I was prone (rarely supine, but mostly sitting up) to "resting in the Lord"?

In transitioning to the next topic, the substance of time, I would like you to consider a person, a dog, a tree, and a rock. They are all subject to the effects of "substance" time. Only the person, the dog, and the tree die, but all four get old and, given enough time (see Chapter 4), cease to exist as such.

I am moderately confident that only the person and the dog perceive time, as I reason that some type of memory needs to be in place for this to occur. Thus, substance time is independent of our perception of time being normal, expanded, or contracted. It continues relentlessly along if we are awake or asleep, driving a sports car at 200 miles per hour or lying in a coma, sentient or not. But it may come as a surprise to you that the person in the sports car will experience a *real* slowing of substance time compared with their stationary counterpart.

As I mentioned previously, when we consider time, we tend to think in terms of seconds, minutes, hours, days, weeks, months, years, decades, and so on. However, these are not actually time but are merely the measure of the passage of time. Just what time is remains the mystery we are trying to elucidate.

Each of us has an innate experience with time that tells us that it seems to be the same wherever we go or whatever we do. Assuming a normally functioning watch, our second hands don't stop or run backwards, hour hands don't skip forward four hours without warning. Or calendars don't skip from March to August without going through the intervening months of April, May, June, and July. We can each attest that our experience has been one of linear progression at a given rate.

No less than Sir Isaac Newton[4] noted the same phenomenon and mandated a requirement for a universal flow of time for what are termed Newtonian physics to be true. And from the event of the publishing of the *Naturalis Principia Mathematica* in 1687, until 1916, a universal standard of time was the accepted state of reality.

Albert Einstein[5] published his theories of special relativity in 1905 and general relativity in 1916. He argued that time, when measured, was not universal but was variable and depended on two factors: the relative speed of one observer to another and the gravitational field.

Those two factors are independent of each other in that, if the two observers are within the same gravitational field, relative motion will govern any time differential. Likewise, if there is no relative motion, then the greater gravitational field of one observer will cause a time differential with the other observer. As far as I know, those two effects could be additive or sub-tractive from each other.

In short, if we have two observers (each with matched and very precise clocks), as one starts to accelerate away from the second (who is in a fixed position and the same gravitational field), then time will start to slow down on the accelerating clock compared to the fixed one.

The differential is very slight at any speed that we can attain, but as we approach the speed of light (186,000 miles per second in a vacuum), time slows to the point of stopping. You might think that the accelerating observer would note things "slowing down," but because it is time itself that has slowed, and the observer is in that reference frame, they are unaware of any change.

This explains something that puzzled me when I first heard it: no matter what speed you travel, even at 185,000 miles per second, you will perceive light as traveling away from you at 186,000 miles per second, the same as if you were standing still. The faster you travel, the more time slows, and it does so in such a way as to keep the speed of light at 186,000 miles per second relative to the observer.

So, if you were a light beam emitted from the sun, how long would it take you to travel to the "edge" of the universe (if such a thing exists)? As time has stopped for you, the trip would be instantaneous. This all sounds like fantasy but has been proven consistent with experimental findings.[6]

Similarly, as one approaches a gravitational field, the greater the gravity, the more time retards. Pierre-Simon Marquis de Laplace (1749–1827) proposed that there might be stars so massive that their gravitational field would prevent even light from escaping them.[7]

It took Karl Schwarzschild (1873–1916), working with Einstein's equations in 1916, to show how spacetime, under the influence of great enough gravity, could be curved into a spherical mass from which light could not escape.[8]

However, it was not until 1967 that the term black hole was popularized by physicist John Wheeler (1911–2008), though it appeared in a 1964 article, "'Black Holes' in Space" by Ann E. Ewing, who heard it at a meeting of the American Association for the Advancement of Science.[9]

It is now believed that at the center of most, if not all, massive spiral galaxies, there exist super massive black holes on the order of up to several billion solar masses. If one were to approach a black hole (a very silly thing to do, by the way!), one would experience a retardation of time[10] similar to that of extreme speed.

However, time would not actually stop until you were crushed out of existence in what is termed a singularity, in which spacetime ceases to exist and only gravity remains. To an outside observer it would seem to take even a longer time than it actually would just because the light escaping to the observer would have been slowed in escaping the local area (called gravitational red shifting) as the subject approached what is known as the event horizon, that point where gravity is so immense that light itself can no longer escape.

So, the question remains: What is "substance" time? I had assumed up until recently that time exists as a discrete thing. As you will read in Chapter 7, "Discovering the Universal Truths," the big bang theory states that everything that exists derives from one primal source or type of energy. By necessity then, time must also be somehow a manifestation of this energy.

I thought this concept might be useful in understanding what is termed the inflationary period of the universe, a concept put forth by physicist Alan Guth in 1980.[11] This theory says that from a period lasting between 10^{-36} to 10^{-32} seconds after the big bang, the universe expanded by a factor of at least 10^{78}.[12]

In effect this says that during that brief time the universe expanded from the atomic level to the size of the currently observable universe. There is good evidence that this is just what happened. (If interested in investigating further, you can search the Internet under "cosmic background microwave radiation.")

I wondered if perhaps expansion represented a phase of the early universe that occurred prior to the primal energy "freezing out" into differing forms, with perhaps dimensionality becoming manifest prior to time per se. However, "prior" itself does seem to mandate the existence of time, so the question becomes oxymoronic, or more probably, just moronic!

Both space and time seem to have had their origin from the same primal burst of energy we refer to as the "big bang", that created the cosmos about 13.8 billion years ago. That singular source is credited with spawning our universe and all that is intrinsic to it; all forms of matter, all forces of nature like light, magnetism and gravity, all the laws that govern how the various components of creation interact, empty space (which actually isn't empty, but that is another discussion), and finally, time itself. After much further consideration, I have begun to entertain the idea that perhaps it is likely space and time (spacetime) are one commodity with two manifestations. I was principally led down this path upon considering how parallel and proportionate the effects of gravity (and therefore acceleration) are on both realities. For example, at 99.99% the speed of light, a clock on a rocket ship will have "slowed down" such that it will show 1 hour has passed while a stationary clock will register the passage of about

70.7 hours. Likewise, the measured length of a 300-foot-long rocket at that speed will seem unchanged to the occupants but will have shrunk to 4.5 feet in length as measured by a stationary observer. Notice how similar the effect of acceleration is on both time dilation and dimensionality. It was not until I had already concluded this that I found that relativistic length contraction and relativistic time dilation are both governed by the Lorentz equations.

That is, length contraction is calculated by the **Lorentz Contraction** $(l' = l \sqrt{1 - v^2/c^2})$ while time dilation follows its reciprocal. $\left(t' = t \middle/ \sqrt{1 - v^2/c^2} \right).$

I sought for a way to illustrate how this could be possible and came up with the concept drawings below. The top figure in Diagram 1 shows two intersecting structures, a two-dimensional plane t (let that t represent time), and a window xyz, as the cartoon of three-dimensional space (height, width, and depth). I added a shaded form that you can either imagine as snake like or a piece of rolled taffy, depending on your preference. In either case, it has taken a sine wave shape. This represents the concept of spacetime. Your perspective as a reader offers the "comprehensive view" of all that there is to spacetime. Using the glasses marked "a.", the viewer has a side view of the structure contained in xyz. Utilizing glasses "b." yields a narrow top view of the object.

Diagram 1

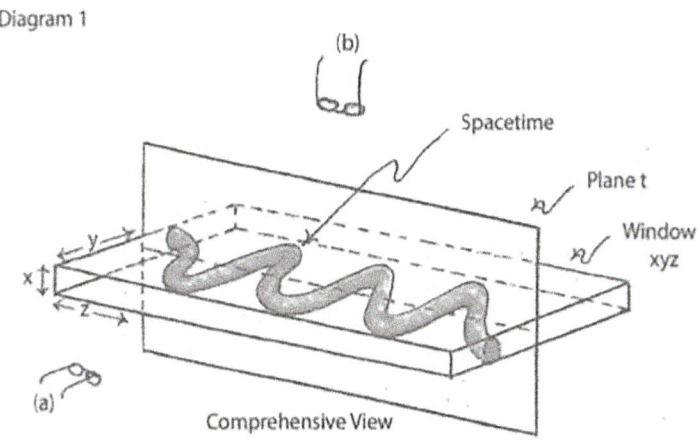

In Diagram 2 we can observe what spacetime looks like from these two vantage points. As seen through xyz, marked (a.), would look to be undulating. However, it might be difficult to determine with certainty if it is round or flat on the visible face. Viewing with glasses "b" is inherently difficult to do. Because we are viewing the plane on edge it appears as a one-dimensional structure. Of course, a single dimensional object cannot really be viewed. To see it, we would need a second dimension to give it some width, so I cheated!

Having resorted to this violation of the concept of planes, the viewer now using the (a.) glasses has a moderately different impression of what they are seeing, compared to that obtained from the vista marked (b.). In fact, this viewer sees something that doesn't seem to faintly resemble either of the preceding visions. There is nothing continuous, only homogenous looking, evenly spaced dashes. All three views, the readers, (a.), and (b.), are accurate and valid in showing what there is to see from those vantage points, however the last two are incomplete.

Diagram 2

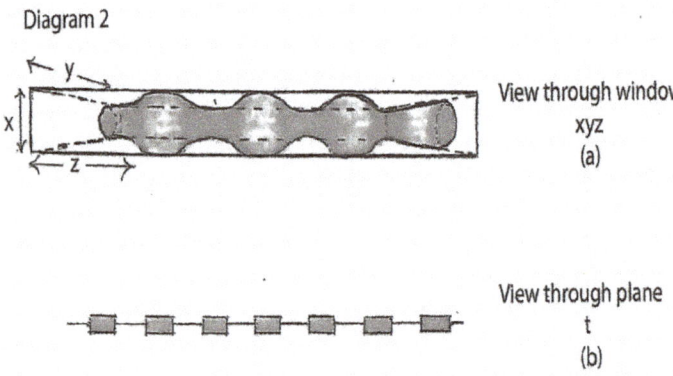

View through window
xyz
(a)

View through plane
t
(b)

In conclusion, I think that from the vantage point of our existence here, we well might be seeing two aspects of a singular item and, not recognizing them as belonging to the very same "object". Instead, we are taking them as being distinct from, instead of intrinsic to, each other. What difference does it make? Well, it might have some bearing on Alan Guth's "Inflation" hypothesis mentioned above but is not likely to positively change your bank account or get you a date on Saturday night. That said, some of you, like me, may find it edifying to contemplate just how intricate and interdependent the relationship of space and time are. I take this as witness to how wonderful and brilliant the God is, who set all of this in place "In the beginning".

Before moving ahead to the next broad topic, I want to consider the possibility of something that intrigues many people, time travel. Your first question will likely be, "Is time travel possible?" To this query I can give a response of, "definitely YES". Not only is it possible, but it is absolutely essential. You and I are both time traveling at this very moment. One might think that after all the practice I've accrued over the past seven decades that I would be very good at it now. Alas, that is not the case. No, I have learned that there is a price to be exacted for traversing time, and my arthritic joints, declining hearing, and the mirror, all give testimony to this.

We discussed earlier how there is such a thing as variable time passage depending on gravity/velocity and the placement of two observers. However, I think what most of us are intrigued with is the ability to visit the past. I am told that the equations for the passage of time work well in forward and in reverse. So, shouldn't we be able to go back? You and I are going to take an imaginary trip. We have met in your living room and your favorite couch has us comfortably seated. I brought my patented, portable time machine along to transport us, and we are ready. We have decided that we would like to return exactly one year through time. We plan to arrive in your living room and on the couch. The machine is all configured and we're off! But did we make it?

The major problem I see here, and it does not seem to depend on if you accept my concept of time or someone else's, or your own, is that I envision no way to travel through just that one dimension, time. Any attempt at time travel necessarily involves concurrent travel through three-dimensional space. You may be a little confused. You are wondering if we are in the same room and on the same couch, how have we moved? What we did not account for is that while your house is stationary on the earth, the earth has been spinning at about 1000 mph, and moving at about 67,000 mph around the Sun, having traversed around 584,000,000 miles the previous year. Meanwhile the Sun has been on its circular journey around the middle of the Milky Way galaxy at 483,000 mph and has traveled about 4.3 billion miles. Therefore, without even accounting for the motion of our galaxy in the universe, that year has witness the earth move about five billion (5,000,000,000) miles from its year ago location. That is a very long journey. I doubt that it will be feasible, at least until we have practical warp drive. That may someday come to be. If interested, check out Alcubierre's warp drive on the internet. However, I perceive a couple of potential hazards to that mode of transport that I will not further discuss here.

Two other hinderances remain. Steps would have to be taken to try to avoid returning through time to the space you currently occupy only to find that, at the time you returned to, that location was already filled by something else. This might best be done in interstellar space. Finally, as far as I know, no one has found any method of inducing that phenomenon.

But what about the forward and backward working computations? I think it is important to not necessarily make the math synonymous with the entity/event described. Math, and in particular quantum mechanics, is a wonderful descriptor of what can go on but is not the actual event. In the same way, I can use words to describe, or a photo to show, a sunset. But neither of those methods is the same as witnessing it personally.

The nature of time, along with many other queries like the composition of dark matter (which makes up about 23 percent of the universe) …and even more mysterious, dark energy (which is said to make up another 73 percent[13] of the substance of the universe)— answers, will probably have to await my arrival in heaven. I shall take some satisfaction in finally knowing. (See Appendix A, "Time, Dimensions, and God: A Mathematician's Perspective.")

So why go into this detail on the subjects of time and energy? My underlying motive is to encourage you to think about things we view as "commonplace" and to appreciate that existence is very complex and governed by intricate principles. I hope to develop this concept further in Chapter 7, "Discovering the Universal Truths", and by doing so gain a greater appreciation for just who God is and why He must exist.

CHAPTER 4

COSMOLOGY: THE NECESSITY OF A NEW HEAVEN AND NEW EARTH

"Then I saw 'a new heaven and a new earth,'
for the first heaven and the first earth had passed
away, and there was no longer any sea."
REVELATION 21:1

But our citizenship is in heaven.
PHILIPPIANS 3:20

After one look at this planet any visitor from outer space would say,
"I want to see the manager."

WILLIAM S. BURROUGHS

Through space the universe encompasses and swallows me up like an
atom; through thought I comprehend the world.
BLAISE PASCAL

One warm and sunny summer afternoon I was in the house working on some project when the doorbell rang. I answered the door and found two men, both well dressed, one about thirty years old and the other probably about seventy. From the brochures I could see in their hands, I had a pretty good idea of what to expect next.

Just as I had thought, they announced they were members of a particular religious group and wanted to give me some literature to read. As I hemmed and hawed and thought to myself that I really must install one of those peepholes in the door so as not to be caught in such a situation, the older one, sensing my hesitancy, said the magic words: "Have you ever considered what heaven will be like?"

That was like throwing a goldfish to a hungry cat! I informed him that I had indeed given thought (for several years now) to the subject. I then asked him, "So, what do you think heaven will be like?"

He eagerly replied that he was sure that he was going to be in heaven and that heaven was, in fact, right here on earth. He was looking forward to forever walking the peaceful earth and watching the flowers and the sky and the ocean and marveling at the beauty of it all.

I contemplated his answer briefly before I responded. A saying from my Uncle Bud crept into my conversation as I told him that while in the short term of a few hundred million years, that might not be too bad, in the long term he would have "driven his ducks to a poor pond."

I went into a brief explanation of the nature of the earth and the solar system. Now, I personally don't care if someone wants to believe in a seven-thousand-year-old earth or a much older earth, just so long as they do not try to make that belief a "make it or break it" deal for knowing God.

In any case, from what evidence science gives us, it appears that the earth is about four and one-half billion years old[1] and is currently a very nice place to live. In fact, it is the only place to live that we are confident of. But from what we are learning by studying stars like our sun, it is not destined to stay that way.

Over the next billion years or so, as the sun continues to convert its primary energy source hydrogen via thermonuclear reaction into helium, it will increase its energy output to earth by about 10 percent.[2] That means more heat. We can expect that sometime in the next 500 million to 750 million years several devastating things will happen. Due to increased temperature, the free carbon dioxide in the atmosphere will decrease in concentration as more of it gets locked up in the oceans in the form of calcium carbonate.[3] At some point there simply will not be enough carbon dioxide in the air, and the 95 percent of plant species on earth that depend on it will cease to exist.[4]

Unfortunately, things deteriorate from there. Relatively shortly (geologically speaking) after that, the increasing temperature will boil off the earth's oceans,[5] leaving earth as a dry and hot place. It will not be much use trying to watch the waves when the oceans have evaporated away. I told him that he will not have any flowers to look at or birds to see when there is no water. As the sun continues to burn, things get a lot worse. About four billion years from now, the sun will have exhausted most of its core hydrogen fuel and will then switch to burning hydrogen in its shell.

I informed him that he might want to invest in dark glasses and lots of SPF creams because at its peak the sun will be putting out over 2,500 times[6] as much light as it does now and, especially with the earth's atmosphere having been blown away by the solar wind, even the best day is not going to be a good one.

I glanced at him and noted that his eyes were starting to glaze over a little, perhaps like yours are right now. But, in any case, I pressed on. Our star currently has a radius of about 500,000 miles, but when it is in full vigor as what is termed a red giant, it will probably have a radius in excess of 100 million miles.[7]

Anyone who knows that the earth is currently 93 million miles from the sun can start to see the problem. At best, if it does not get pulled into the sun by gravitational forces and tidal forces in the sun's atmosphere, the earth's surface will again be totally molten. Swimming won't be an option.

I cannot help but think of 2 Peter 3:7 and 10: "By the same word the present heavens and earth are reserved for fire.... The heavens will disappear with a roar; the elements will be destroyed by fire, and the earth and everything done in it will be laid bare."

Of course, the sun does not stay a red giant forever. As the outer layers of hydrogen are depleted, more helium falls to the core of the star. The red giant probably shrinks somewhat for a time. The increasing helium mass at the center starts to heat up due to gravitational contraction, and this results in what is termed a helium flash.[8]

For our purposes it can be thought of as the "hot flash" as the sun undergoes "the change" from middle to late-middle age. This helium flash allows for helium to start to fuse with helium. After approximately a mere billion years as a red giant, the sun will puff off its outer layers. When there is not sufficient helium left to burn (fuse into carbon and oxygen), it will then collapse down to what is termed a white dwarf.

Think of this as an intensely glowing very dense ball not much larger than earth but with half of the total mass of our sun, roughly 165,000 earths. At that mass and diameter, it will have a density of about 32,000 pounds per cubic inch.[9]

If this planet does manage to survive that long, it will be essentially a burned cinder with no atmosphere, circling a distant dwarf star that no longer provides enough energy[10] to warm the barren rock that used to be called earth. With the "hot spell" finally over, surface temperatures here should settle slightly above a rather chilly -459.67 degrees Fahrenheit, or absolute zero, as it is termed. That is roughly the same temperature as the cold stare some dimwitted husband may expect from his spouse after making a derogatory remark about the dinner she just prepared.

If we could visit the earth at that point, we would find it to be so alien there would be no way we could recognize it. If there is any type of atmosphere left, it would be unbreathable. There is nothing to see but blackened rock, and none of the earth's most notable features, from the oceans to the Himalayas, are likely to leave significant remnants. There are no people, animals, plants, bacteria, or viruses.

There is no evidence of boundaries that formed nations or that people existed or fought and died trying to claim one spot of sand and rock from someone else. There is not even a fossil record to suggest that this charred rock ever hosted life. Most of what is remaining is difficult to see since the earth is bathed in perpetual and unending night. Even if you look to the sky, nothing is likely to look familiar. There is a good chance that the moon will not exist.[11]

The Milky Way is currently on a collision course with our big sister, the Andromeda Galaxy. That collision starts in about four billion years and should be complete by six billion to seven billion years from now.[12] Do not expect our constellations to look remotely familiar after that. The writer of Ecclesiastes was correct when he wrote, "'Meaningless! Meaningless' says the Teacher. 'Everything is meaningless!'" (Ecclesiastes 12:8).

I could see that I had probably ruined some of his idyllic images, so I did not bother to tell him the rest of the story for fear of depressing him. In any case, the two men thanked me for my time and ended up not leaving me anything to read. I do wish them Godspeed in finding heaven.

Now for those of you who want to know the rest of the story of the universe, as we currently understand it, consider taking a Prozac and read on. Things only get worse. It is likely that our sun will have bequeathed this terrestrial ball some residual havoc by having acted as it did. The outer planets like Jupiter and Saturn will quite possibly have had their voluminous atmospheres boiled away, leaving their rocky cores.

There will likely be destabilization of orbits of not only the planets but of things beyond, like objects that exist at the periphery of our solar system in what is called the Oort cloud.[13] This may bring about heavenly bodies of substantial size (comets, asteroids) raining into the central part of our solar system, and that means significant potential impact.[14] Combine this with gravitational changes and the chances of the cooling ember earth surviving are small.

But let us take another line to see if there is a way to temporarily avert this catastrophe. If you were to move to one of the moons of Jupiter when the sun is in red-giant phase, there might be a chance of having a temperate life for a while. We know that there are vast reserves of water available there,[15] but you still would have to deal with the big chill to follow.

How about if we became highly technologically advanced and did something truly radical? What if we were able to move the earth to a different star, one that was much more stable. If our sun has a lifespan of about 11 billion years from inception to white dwarf,[16] we might consider relocation to an orbit around what is termed a red dwarf.

Red dwarf. Now that sounds like a diminutive person who happens to arrive one day earlier in the sunnier southern climes on the beach of the land of Oz. This contrasts with a brown dwarf (you guessed it—he spent the entire summer at the beach). Astronomically speaking, a brown dwarf is essentially a gas giant (no, not a politician), that is, a planet like Jupiter or Saturn except several times the size of Jupiter.

The difference between these two dwarf brothers is that the red one has a mass about one-tenth of the sun, and his brown sibling a mass of just under that amount. At that size, "brownie" is just short of the mass and gravity that it would take to cause sufficient pressure (roughly 10 billion times our atmospheric pressure) and heat at its core (around 10 million degrees Kelvin or 18 million degrees Fahrenheit) to start and sustain the fusion of hydrogen atoms to form helium that powers the main sequence of stars.

"Red" just met that threshold and ignited in a long and slow burn. It may seem paradoxical but, sadly, much like many Hollywood versions, the bigger the star, the shorter its lifespan. This is simply because the bigger stars will fuse more hydrogen to helium (burn hotter) and go through their primary fuel supply much faster. Red dwarfs do not burn as hot as our sun, but they can give off significant energy, and their gravitation is such that it might be possible to bring a planet into a stable orbit at a hospitable distance (habitable zone). As opposed to the sun with a 9-billion-year lifespan in main phase, a red dwarf has an average lifespan of probably more than 10 trillion (10,000 billion) years.[17]

This is a relatively good short-term solution, and one could even go from dwarf to dwarf (kind of like Snow White) for some time. However, eventually the universe will stop making red dwarfs and stars in general. Even if we manage to find our way to the last star and bask in its waning light, a final dilemma—one from which there is no escape—awaits.

Allow me a short digression to set the stage for this discussion. I have had some interest in astronomy from as far back as I can remember. I recall lying in my dad's big sleeping bag in the back yard between my two older brothers on a summer night. I grew up in Bend, Oregon, where, on the east side of the Cascades at 3,600 feet of elevation, one can expect frost twelve months a year. I did not mind being assigned that least-desired place, between my two siblings—if I remembered to go to the bathroom before they settled in for the night. Anyway, as I laid there listening to the regular slow breathing on either side of me, I recall the crisp cold night air on my skin and the brightness of the stars. I remember feeling as if I could fall into the sky.

There was no astronomy in high school. The only "stars" there were on the football and basketball teams. It only took me one term in undergraduate school, having taken an art class, to conclude that I might refrain from taking classes in subjects that I liked for fear that they would lose their appeal.

It wasn't until I had finished medical school, my internship, and my residency and had been in practice for several years that I was tempted to revisit the possibility of doing more than reading astronomy magazines and science fiction. At last, I enrolled in a night class that met once a week at a local community college.

Perhaps it was just not having the pressure of a grade to consider. Maybe it was just that it was such a good diversion from the stresses of my day job, but I found this class to be thoroughly enjoyable.

While I was in that class, I remember the professor bringing up the question about whether we lived in an open, flat, or closed universe. An *open* universe is one that, since its beginning, has been expanding and will continue to expand forever. A *flat* universe is one that will expand to just a certain degree and then run out of energy, remaining stable in its state. A *closed* universe is one that will expand but at some point, will run out of expansive energy then start to collapse under the influence of gravity, finally falling back to the antithesis of the big bang, called the big crunch.

Albert Einstein had concluded that the universe was most likely an open one, but it was not until the work of astronomer Edwin Hubble[18] (for whom the Hubble space telescope is named) at Mount Wilson that his belief was given some degree of confirmation. Hubble showed that the farther galaxies are from us, the faster they are moving away from us. It is beyond the scope of this treatise to discuss how this was ascertained and the use of what are termed standard candles and red shift. But the concepts are reasonably straightforward.

For many decades after that time, the debate concerned the rate of this expansion, called the Hubble constant. A value of about 70 km per second per megaparsec is the currently accepted value. This means that for every megaparsec (or 3.26 million light-years) that a galaxy is away from us, it is accelerating away at rate of an additional 70 kilometers per second.

It was not until 1998 that a most remarkable discovery was made. It now appears that not only are we in an open universe, but the rate at which the universe is expanding is accelerating![19] So is the Hubble constant going to remain a constant? It seems to me that while the Hubble constant is currently valid, as time progresses and acceleration of the universe continues, the Hubble number will also have to increase. There are theories involving "dark energy" as to why this acceleration is happening. But at this point, the basis for this phenomenon is seemingly beyond anyone's understanding or guess.

I will now skip forward a mere 22 billion (22 x 10 to the 9th) years to the conclusion of this cosmologic acceleration scenario. The ultimate result of this process is *that* the forces of this acceleration will, at first, tear apart clusters of galaxies, then galaxies, then solar systems, then planets, then smaller items, even down to the atomic and subatomic level. This is called the big rip. [20] If the universe were to survive this and continue to accelerate, as the universal expansion approached 186,000 miles per second, would time stop?

If the big rip is not correct, then there are other theories, like the "big freeze."[21] After 100 trillion (10^{14}) years the stars have all burned out. We know that matter decays and by 10^{34} years there is essentially nothing but an eternity of a cold, endless void with no light or sound, just some faint background radiation and subatomic particles flitting in and out of existence.

Now how is that for boring? The "big crunch"[22] involves the expansion instead slowing and then everything falling back together to one point in the next 100 billion years or so.

All the above scenarios suppose that God simply lets the clock run down and does not play His wild card of intervening personally and flashing the "game over" sign.

Of course, He has the option and power to intercede as He wishes. One may certainly make a good case for this, citing both Old and New Testament sources.

Isaiah 65:17: "See, I will create new heavens and a new earth. The former things will not be remembered, nor will they come to mind."

The book of Revelation has a fair amount to say about cosmological events: "The first angel sounded his trumpet, and there came hail and fire mixed with blood, and it was hurled down upon the earth. A third of the earth was burned up, a third of the trees were burned up, and all the green grass was burned up. The second angel sounded his trumpet, and something like a huge mountain, all ablaze, was thrown into the sea. A third of the sea turned into blood, a third of the living creatures in the sea died, and a third of the ships were destroyed. The third angel sounded his trumpet and a great star, blazing like a torch, fell from the sky on a third of the rivers and on the springs of water—the name of the star is Wormwood. A third of the waters turned bitter, and many people died from the waters that had become bitter [radioactive?]. The fourth angel sounded his trumpet, and a third of the sun was struck, a third of the moon, and a third of the stars, so that a third of them turned dark. A third of the day was without light, and also a third of the night." (8:7–12)

When reading that Revelation passage, did visions of near-earth asteroids or perhaps a comet that had ventured close to a large planetary body and been fractured into pieces come to your mind? In 1994, pieces of that heavenly body designated comet Shoemaker-Levy rained down on Jupiter over a six-day period. Some of those impacts punched earth-sized holes in the atmosphere.[23] What do you suppose would happen if one fragment was to hit in one of the earth's oceans and another was to hit on the land?

Revelation 21:1–3 says: "Then I saw a new heaven and a new earth, for the first heaven and the first earth had passed away, and there was no longer any sea. I saw the Holy City, the new Jerusalem, coming down out of heaven from God, prepared as a bride beautifully dressed for her husband. And I heard a loud voice from the throne saying, 'Look! God's dwelling place is now among the people, and he will dwell with them.'"

Does this future destruction implicitly mean the entire universe or simply the earth and its environs? I can imagine it either way. Since we are essentially confined to earth for the foreseeable future, it makes little difference. Like other nonessentials of the peripheral issues of Christianity, I think it fun to speculate on but pointless to argue about it. When we get to heaven, then we can say, "Well, you were right and I was wrong," or vice versa. My guess is that once we have arrived there, we won't much care either way.

The words of Oliver Hardy[24] to Stan Laurel[25] come ringing to my mind, "Well, here's another fine mess you've gotten us into." I am afraid this world and even this universe do not offer lasting refuge for any of us who would be immortal. For what is even 10 to the 250th years in the scope of eternity?

Nothing more than the very beginning.

CHAPTER 5

SEX

"You make known to me the path of life; you will fill me with joy in your presence, with eternal pleasures at your right hand."
PSALM 16:11

I remember the first time I had sex—I kept the receipt.
GROUCHO MARX

Sex is emotion in motion.
MAE WEST

Sex without love is a meaningless experience, but as far as meaningless experiences go it's pretty damn good.
WOODY ALLEN

Being a sex symbol is a heavy load to carry, especially when one is tired, hurt, and bewildered.
MARILYN MONROE

I know that nothing spurs curiosity more quickly than the three letters above, given in that specific order, so I decided to put them in capital letters to make it easy for people to find this chapter.

As you read in *the* chapter about historical perspective on heaven, beliefs differ among and within religions about what part sex may play in the afterlife. While I implied in that chapter that there is good reason to doubt that it is the focal point of life in the hereafter, it is deemed an important aspect of existence by enough people to consider its place in the eternal.

I think that religion in general, and Christianity in particular, is often perceived as somehow being not only opposed but even appalled by the concept of sex. Of course, this is not the case. If the Christian perspective on sex differs, it is only with respect to the overall importance sex should play in one's own life and within the context of relationship with others.

While a true hedonist[1] would place it, along with food, drink, and other forms of pleasure as the ultimate goal of life, Christians should see it as a useful and enjoyable pastime to further our relationships with our spouses and ultimately learn more about God. Sex was one of my first clues that He might have a sense of humor. Rather than shun the topic, Christian and non-Christian parents have common ground in wanting to give our own offspring what we deem a proper perspective on sex. And, just like all parents who try to impart this to their offspring, we often fall short of 100 percent success.

Once more I shall refer to my personal experience of being a father. On one occasion in 1995 or so, while driving back over to the Willamette Valley from visiting my family in Bend, Oregon, my wife sat beside me, and it appeared that our five children were all asleep. At that time, there was a certain high-ranking politician who ultimately would prove that even a Rhodes scholar can be tripped up by simple things in the English language. His particular conundrum would come in trying to discern what the definition of is is. A voice arose from the back seat of the van, "Hey, Dad, how close do you have to sleep to a girl for her to get pregnant?"

My precocious eight-year-old Michael had struck again. Now, I had always intended to have "the talk" with my kids, but I did not envision trying to do it by yelling from the front seat to the back, nor had I anticipated giving it to a third grader. Nonetheless, the gauntlet had been slapped across my cheek. I responded, "Son, you know that is a great question. But right now, I am kind of busy driving, and I can't hear you all that well, so why don't you remember that question and ask me again when we get home."

I admit that I was probably exercising cowardice here as much as caution and would not have been at all disappointed if he had simply forgotten the question for at least a couple more years. Such was not to be the case. Having arrived at home, and with the rest of the kids gone to bed, the question was again put forth. I determined that if I was going to delve into this topic now, it was going to be a thorough exploration of the entire subject.

I proceeded to launch into what must have been 20–25 minutes of anatomy, physiology, the concept of love, morality, and consequence of sex. He was very attentive. When I finally was satisfied with my response to his query, I was quite pleased and patting myself on the back, thinking that every father should have such a comprehensive talk with their children. Not wishing to leave any gray areas, I asked him if he had any questions.

He stood there for a second and then responded, "Well, yes.

How do you do it?"

I said, "Michael, what do you mean? I just spent the last half-hour telling you how to do it!"

"No, no, I mean, like, do you just walk up to a girl and pull her pants down or what?"

Picking up my deflated ego from the floor and recalling some recent news articles, I responded, "No, son. You don't just go up and pull her pants down. At least not unless you are the president or at least a senator."

I am very sure that Satan would like to take credit for sex. However, sex is not his invention but God's.[2, 3] It was intended to be extremely enjoyable and not just to be used for procreation, though He probably did consider the pleasure factor when planning to get people to reproduce in the first place.

As my son David said at the pre-pubertal age of 11, when he was finally given "the talk," "Before this I thought I might actually get married someday. I was wrong! Kissing the girl is only the *second* grossest thing!" Now at age 33, and married, with two children, I am confident that he has been able to move beyond his initial reluctance.

Beyond the physical pleasure, it is intended to give a bonding of spirit, a reassurance of commitment, a way of drawing a couple together in a special relationship. I will not over-spiritualize things here, but I do believe that there was intended to be something mystical about this union. I doubt that God would have devoted an entire book of the Bible (Song of Solomon) essentially to sex without good reason.

While these are all valid reasons for the existence of sex, I do not believe they are well represented in the world at large. We see sex used as a weapon of influence or power, as a form of abuse, as recreation, as a rationale for harming others, and, most of all, as a marketing tool to sell anything from the obvious magazines to automobiles. Has there ever been a cover of *Cosmopolitan* in the past 30 years that did not have "sex" written on it somewhere? Does Victoria have any more secrets?

"This car is sexy!" Really? "Hey, nice set of tail pipes you got there, baby." I guess that it might be legitimately used for something that mimics the human form, but using it to sell beer? Who is, at least initially, attracted to a person because they are shaped like a can or even bottle of beer?

Of course, whether the sales pitch is for alcohol, perfume, clothes, or cars, the not-so-subliminal message is that if you buy and use this product, you are more likely to "get laid." God engineered us so we could have sex in the first place. He put a lot of design detail into giving us a way not only to reproduce but also to derive pleasure. The thing is that He wanted it to be under the best of circumstances, where there would be no worry of contraction of disease, no guilt, no wounded feelings, and no fear of having unwanted children. When children are the result, He wanted them to be raised in a stable and loving atmosphere where the parents are committed to each other and those children. Given that, should we expect that there might be sex beyond this life? In order to sort out why it may or may not exist in that realm, we need to know a little more about what makes sex, "sexy."

At the risk of making this topic a little boring, I think a cursory look at the biochemistry and neuroanatomy of sex and pleasure can shed some light on this subject. I have heard it said that 90 percent of sex takes place from the eyebrows up. That is, physiologically speaking, a seemingly valid statement. So, falling back on my medical roots, I note a few facts.[4]

Big surprise, the brain is an incredibly complex organ in structure, function, and interaction. What I present here is vastly "dumbed down"—and thus at a level where I can better understand it.

The portion of the brain that I am discussing here is best thought of as that part that generally is termed the pleasure center. This is mostly encapsulated in what is known as the limbic system, which is seated deep within the brain and is thought to be the source of those drives that help to ensure the survival of the individual and, thus, the species. It helps mediate things like feeding stimuli, memory, emotion, motivation, and sexual behavior.

The primary foci or nuclei, as they are termed, are located in the hippocampus, amygdala, hypothalamus, nucleus accumbens, ventral tegmental area, and other structures. Their function is influenced by hormones and the rest of the nervous system.

For instance, if a post-menopausal female comes in complaining of a lack of libido and there are no contraindications, then a physician might consider prescribing a low dose testosterone. I have had several wives (and their husbands!) give me their enthusiastic "Thanks!" after trying this.

Yet, we are not total slaves to our hormones. Our cerebral cortex, that part of the brain where the intellect and reason reside, can override, or modify stimulation of the limbic system. Learning to activate this control is one of the principal challenges of becoming an adult and starts in adolescence.

I remember on one occasion, riding in the car with my brothers and my (at that time) seventy-five-year-old dad. My oldest brother remarked that he had been doing some reading and that there had been some research done to show that humans tended to have times when, like baboons, they would go into "heat." Pop commented that he recalled when this happened to him. He stated that he was about 13 years old at the time and that he was still waiting for it to end.

The portions of the limbic system are structurally connected by what is termed the median forebrain bundle, and the main chemical used to transmit signals along this bundle is dopamine. That is, dopamine is used to pass the signals along from one nerve to the next at the junction between the nerves. Stimulation of the structures within this system is associated with an increase in either the amount of dopamine released or change in how long the dopamine is allowed to remain in the junction before being removed, thus ending the signal. Activation of this area causes a feeling of wellness, decreased anxiety, satisfaction, and of course, pleasure. Disruption of any of these structures can have significant impact on the remainder of the system.

The nucleus accumbens is especially important in that it appears to be the primary target site of drugs of abuse, which have the final common effect of increasing the amount of dopamine stimulation at the nerve junctions. Other neurotransmitters such as serotonin, GABA, and endogenous opiates (endorphins) also influence this system in either a positive or negative manner. Oh, and that first cup of coffee in the morning to get you going, guess what effect the caffeine has on the system? Yup, you guessed it, increased dopamine.

Studies have been done where electrodes are placed into the nucleus accumbens. The experimental animal, usually a rat (though I am sure that consideration has been given to using other animal models that lack higher cerebral function, like teenage boys) is given a way of initiating self-stimulation by actuating these electrodes. That is, a system is set up where the subject may cause stimulation by pushing a lever.

As previously mentioned, this portion of the brain was designed to help ensure survival. However, animals will engage in self-stimulation to the extent they will forego food and water to the point of starvation. It does not take very long when looking at pictures of people who have become addicted to crack cocaine to recognize similar results in humans who subject themselves to that drug.

If we examine what is known to happen in the brain at the time of orgasm, we find that there is a sudden flood of a variety of neurotransmitters, including norepinephrine, oxytocin, vasopressin, nitric oxide, prolactin and our old friend, serotonin. Of course, dopamine levels go racing and, hopefully, a good time is had by all.

Oxytocin and vasopressin are involved in the feeling of social attachment in human mating. Prolactin is interesting in that it is associated with the feeling of sexual satisfaction. It also is chiefly responsible for post-coital (after sex) drowsiness. This is the same hormone that is responsible for producing breast milk. Its production is increased by breast stimulation. Any moms out there ever fall asleep while breast-feeding? You probably had good reason to be tired anyway, but this was your "nightcap."

Interestingly, prolactin and dopamine are mutually antagonistic. Prolactin causes the refractory period after orgasm.

Like a married couple, during a disagreement, they tend to counteract each other. I can just hear their conversation now. "Good time" dopamine (Dopey) says, "Come on, baby, what do you say we do it again?" Prolactin doesn't take long in responding, "Not again! I don't feel like it, and I'm too tired."

Okay, no more boring anatomy or physiology. Well, maybe just a little more. Of course, we do not know exactly what our resurrection state entails with respect to our physical make-up.

While I do not think that Isaiah 40:31 ("but those who hope in the LORD will renew their strength. They will soar on wings like eagles") and 65:25 ("The wolf and the lamb will feed together, and the lion will eat straw like the ox") are necessarily to be taken literally, I think they do point to the fact that there will likely be fundamental changes in our physiology and appetites.

It is possible this may include our sexual desires as well. It is conceivable that sex as we know it could end up being a non sequitur. For reasons that I hope to go into when I discuss the interpersonal aspects of existence in heaven, I have good cause to suspect that all our relationships there are going to be far more profound than any that we currently experience on earth, including marriage.

Given our "new nature," which I will explore in greater extent in the following chapters, if there is sex in heaven, it will be far superior to any experienced here. Should I be wrong in this assumption, then I would surmise that it is only because sex would be replaced by something else far more grand, pleasurable, and overall enjoyable.

As I said earlier, God is the one who thought up sex in the first place and made it as desirable as it is. Anyone who passes up the opportunity to go to heaven by making worldly sex their "god" is, again as my colorful uncle would say, driving their ducks to the worst pond possible. Who in the literal hell do you think thought up erectile dysfunction, anorgasmia, venereal disease, and abortion? If you really want the ultimate in pleasurable pastimes, you can just go straight to heaven!

CHAPTER 6

SPECIAL ABILITIES AND SENSATIONAL SENSES

"After that, we who are still alive and are left
will be caught up together with them in the clouds to
meet the Lord in the air."
1 THESSALONIANS 4:17

*If I say, "Surely the darkness will hide me and the light become
night around me,"
even the darkness will not be dark to you;
the night will shine like the day, for the darkness is as light to you.*
PSALM 139:11–12

As we advance in life, we learn the limits of our abilities.
HENRY FORD

*All our knowledge begins with the senses, proceeds then to the
understanding, and ends with reason.
There is nothing higher than reason.*
IMMANUEL KANT

I f you ask people what they think will be fun to do in
heaven, most mention having special abilities. Probably the
new capability that I personally most fantasize about is the

capacity to fly. I remember as a boy of three or so going out on a warm summer afternoon and laying on the grass in the front yard, content just to stare up into the deep blue sky. I remember seeing what I would later learn was a "con" (condensation) trail of a jet as it traveled from north to south across that smooth, brilliant sapphire ocean. I don't think I have ever lost the desire to fly since then.

In the old days, when television was new and all three stations signed off in the later hours of the evening, I recall a video they used to play right before the test pattern showed up to officially bring the broadcast day to a close.

This one or two-minute clip showed a jet fighter winging its way through the clouds while some music played softly in the background. Then a deep and melodious voice would recite a poem by John Gillespie Magee Jr.[1] called "High Flight." It was the first poem I ever learned to recite that was not a nursery rhyme. All these years later it still rings in my memory:

> *Oh! I have slipped the surly bonds of earth*
> *And danced the sky on laughter silvered wings;*
> *Sunward I have climbed and joined the tumbling mirth*
> *Of sun-split clouds and done a hundred things*
> *You have not dreamed of—*
> *Wheeled and soared and swung high in the sunlit silence.*
> *Hov'ring there, I've chased the shouting wind along*
> *And flung my eager craft through footless halls of air.*
> *Up, up the long delirious burning blue*
> *I've topped the windswept heights with easy grace,*
> *Where never lark or even eagle flew;*
> *And, while with silent, lifting mind I have trod the un-trespassed*
> *sanctity of space Put out my hand, and touched the face of God.*

When I was in undergraduate school, I went so far as to take a ground school class and even took and passed my FAA test. Alas, my impecunious state never allowed me to take any flying lessons so I think that my first real taste of flight will have to be in heaven. It will be so much more fun without an airplane anyway.

I have always envisioned sliding along effortlessly on the warm wind in a state of total bliss toward the setting sun. I could do that for a long time, but I know that I could not do it forever. No, eventually I would have grown too accustomed to the fresh breeze in my face, the sun displaying its array of hues. Besides, I would probably get hungry and need to take a bathroom break. You would not want me flying overhead when I needed to do that.

While I am sure that other special abilities would likewise be entertaining for a good while (if God can give me the ability to fly, perhaps He can do something even more miraculous and give me a decent golf swing!), eventually the most exciting of circumstances can turn blasé. Something more is going to be needed beyond my being pretty much as I am but with some special new abilities. Perhaps something can be done to enhance the abilities that I currently possess.

A major impediment I ascertain to our ability to avoid the tedium of the timeless is the limited nature of our senses. To try to put some scale to the magnitude of our infirmity, let us first ponder our sight, which is one of our keenest senses. Vision is the ability to perceive electromagnetic radiation over a range of wavelengths.

For all practical purposes, our vision is limited to the bandwidth extending from 3.8×10^{-7} to 7.40×10^{-7} meter. [2] These wavelengths will give us our palette of colors: red, orange, yellow, green, blue, indigo, and violet.

Now, let us consider the total breadth of the electromagnetic spectrum, which spans from radio waves where each wave is 1000 meters (10 soccer fields) in length to gamma rays at 0.000000000001 meters, or one-trillionth of a meter. For comparison's sake, it is 1.35 trillion meters to the sun from the earth. If we take a meter and reduce it by a commensurate amount, that should provide a smattering of the scale involved.

Thus, we note that our ability to absorb the visible information available amounts to only 0.0000000000001 percent of the potential. Now just imagine the new vistas that await when all of this becomes "visible" to us. I would hazard to guess that when the psalmist wrote the psalm cited above, while very much believing what he was writing, he would have had difficulty conceptualizing how such a thing would be possible.

During the past one hundred years, we have been gifted with insight into the veracity of such a claim. Today we do not wince at the thought of infrared images, as I dare say that most of us have seen them printed in magazines or played on television. Perhaps you have purchased (at no great expense) a device with which you can do this yourself—night-vision binoculars.

If we examine the information available to us from our numerous scientific websites, we will find pictures taken in the wavelengths ranging from radio waves to ultraviolet or X-ray spectrums. Scientists are ever refining pictures taken in the cosmic background microwave radiation.[3,4] These pictures show the residue of an event that appears to have taken place about 13.8 billion years ago, the creation of the universe.

Thus, we have dealt with spectrum of potential "light" to us. We have not yet touched the other aspect of sight, visual acuity. In short, this means the sharpness with which we can see an object at a distance, near or far, extremely large to extremely small.

As humans we have set a standard visual acuity of normalcy at 20/20. If you have this visual acuity, it means that at a distance of 20 feet you can see what is normal for a human to see at that distance. If you are far sighted you may have 20/15, or even 20/10; i.e., you can see at 20 feet what the normal person can see at 15 feet or 10 feet. If you are near sighted, you may have a visual acuity of 20/40 or 20/60 or more. In these cases, you would see at 20 feet what the normal person would see at 40 feet or 60 feet.

A currently accepted medical definition of blindness is a visual acuity of worse than 20/200. When I met my wife-to-be, her visual acuity reportedly was 20/800 without the use of her contact lenses. As you might guess, I never let her put in her contacts until after we were married. No longer could I reassure her, "Oh, yes, dear, I look *just* like Tom Selleck."

Now let us consider what is available in the animal world. Think back to the last time you took a commercial airline flight. When you were at altitude, how much luck would you have trying to see an individual house or even a football field?

Let us now ponder the common buzzard. Not something you usually think of in the context of "awesome," is it? However, its retina (the light receiving membrane lining the inside of the back of the eye) contains one million photoreceptors per square millimeter.

In addition to that, the lens of the eye is the kind of thing that would make the good folks at Canon green with envy. With that combination, this bird can reportedly see a small rodent from a height of fifteen thousand feet![5]

One could argue that God either got a little over-enthusiastic or was just plain showing off when He engineered this structure. I mean, when you were on that airplane flight, do you remember looking out the window and seeing any buzzards floating around?

Given the facts that at that altitude the atmospheric pressure is about half that at sea level [6] and the temperature is about 30 degrees centigrade (54 degrees Fahrenheit) colder than the temperature at ground level,[7] the creature should be easy to spot. Simply look for a large bird wearing a custom-made sleeveless sweater, flapping its wings at a frantic pace, wearing a small oxygen mask, and all the while staring at the ground, probably thinking to itself that life would have been much simpler had it been hatched a canary. At any rate, the fact that this bird has the capability of that acuity at that distance is indeed remarkable.

Looking beyond the animal model, we have the current technological achievement of telescopes. God has gifted man with incredible ingenuity, and its fruit is indeed wondrous. The Hubble Space Telescope was placed into orbit in 1990. This remarkable instrument has revolutionized astronomy by being placed outside of the influence of the earth's atmosphere. The atmosphere, with its eddies and currents, is what makes stars appear to twinkle. If you were to view the heavens from the space shuttle, you would not see any shimmering of the stars.

The HST has a primary mirror of about two and one-half meters in diameter. When speaking of telescopes, we no longer use the term *acuity* and instead use the term *resolution*. This refers to the ability of the telescope to distinguish two objects as being separate from each other at a distance. The Hubble is said to have a resolution of 0.05 arc seconds at optical wavelengths. This number probably does not mean much to you unless you happen to be well versed in astronomy. Another way of saying this is that it has the capability to distinguish between two fireflies placed one meter apart from a distance of 5,000 km (3,000 mi).[8] Larger orbital telescopes such as the James Webb Space Telescope are arriving. This telescope is said to be able to detect the infrared signature from a bee at a distance of the earth to the moon.

If we recognize our visual abilities as limited, then our other senses border on pathetic. Hearing, our ability to sense sound, is our capacity to register sound waves at different frequencies and intensities. More specifically, it is the perception of the motion of molecules.

In our experience this takes place most of the time in air, but it also takes place in other substances such as water or metal. These molecules are set in motion by some force that is itself vibrating. The motion of the molecules in the object then imparts this energy to the surrounding medium, such as air, by bumping into them. Those atoms then bump into the next atom in line, and the cycle repeats itself, much as the motion of a train engine is sequentially transmitted to the following cars. Because the original object vibrates back and forth, it will exert first more (positive) pressure during the outward excursion of the vibration followed by less (negative) pressure during the inward excursion.

This sets up patterns of pressure that are waves. As with the ripples in a pond, the pattern radiates from the point of origin. A greater energy will produce more violent motion, causing larger waves that we perceive as loudness. Since there is more energy, it can travel farther before being dissipated.

The faster the vibration, the higher the frequency (rapidity) with which the waves occur, which we will hear as higher in tone. These vibrations can be transmitted at different speeds, depending on the medium through which they are traveling. In air at sea level, we expect the speed to be on the order of 1,125 feet per second.[9]

In water, due to the greater density of the conducting substance, this rate of propagation increases to about 4,750 feet per second.[10] In steel, the sound will travel at about 20,000 feet per second.[11] Of course, this vibratory energy would mean nothing to us if we did not possess some means by which to sense it.

Ears—everybody seems to have them. But, except for the occasional urge to adorn them with bangles and baubles, we don't tend to give them much attention, until they start to malfunction. They deserve a much higher degree of respect.

When the waves of pressure enter the ear canal, they encounter a thin layer of tissue known as the tympanic membrane, or eardrum. This tissue is vibrated by the successive waves. That motion is transmitted to three small bones that fit together and transmit the energy to a fluid-filled cavity where the fluid is set in motion, again in the form of waves. These then stimulate nerve endings lining this cavity, and the information is transmitted to the brain, where we interpret it as sound.

As with vision, our ability to perceive sound has definite constraints with a range from about 20 cycles per second up to 20,000 cycles per second.[12] That is respectable but fails to explain the phenomenon of sounds that inexplicably go missing and, in doing so, cause no small consequence. (Consider the hapless male who in all honestly states, "But dear, I didn't hear you say to put the toilet seat back down.")

Surely, our fellow mammal the dolphin, with its acoustic range of 20 to 150,000 cycles per second,[13] is not subject to this same foible. Ladies, if you want to avoid all possibility of encountering the "toilet trap," I encourage you to consider marrying a dolphin.

One of our more poorly rendered faculties is smell. From the time I was small, I was told that dogs have an incredible sense of smell. The amount of their brain that is dedicated to this function dwarfs what humans possess, even if not allowing for the difference in size of the human brain and the dog brain.

Indeed, it is said that the canine ability to detect aroma may be up to ten million times keener than our own.[14] (For my part, I find this difficult to believe. Because of my relatively gifted sense of sight, I have had opportunity to see where dogs often choose to place their noses! Even with my handicapped abilities to detect aroma, there is no way that I would knowingly subject my proboscis to such odoriferous environs.)

If the ability of "man's best friend" to sense molecules in the air is prodigious, then the ability of the silkworm moth is downright astounding. This diminutive creature can detect pheromones (sexual hormones) in concentrations of as low as one molecule per ten quadrillion molecules of air. This allows it to smell a potential mate from up to 11 kilometers (6.8 miles) away.[15]

However, every ability has a potential downside. Imagine our well-intended friend Mr. Moth out looking for his soul mate when he detects the faintest hint of her on the passing summer breeze. Instantly he knows that the love of his life exists, and he must find her.

Casting all other priorities aside, he sets off, circling at first, to see if he can detect any increase in this "love potion" in one direction or another. Finally, he has his heading and is off! Heeding not the dangers of marauding birds, ensuing darkness, and a headwind, he battles along to find his one true love. His wings beat on stroke after stroke after stroke, hour after hour, her scent growing ever stronger and now flooding his chemical receptors with her very essence.

Finally, almost totally exhausted, a goodly portion of his life spent in his passionate quest, he spies her and marshals on the last few inches—only to find that, given the distance the pheromones were carried by that selfsame headwind that he had to battle all the way back, she is now the mother of 253 offspring and the grandmother of 63,250 more!

There are other amazing senses, such as the pit viper being able to detect temperature changes on the order of 0.002 degrees centigrade,[16] or scorpions to being able detect air flow as low as 0.047 miles per hour.[17] Then there are abilities of which we have virtually no personal experience, such as the detection of electrical fields, magnetic fields, and gravity (other than noting that it is harder to get out of bed every year).

Let us imagine that we are now, in our heavenly state, in possession of all these capabilities but to a degree unprecedented even in the above examples. Surely that would open realms for us to explore that would keep us occupied for many, many years. But what are many, many years in the scope of eternity, other than "just the beginning"? So, we find that we need more to escape the trap of boredom. But what? Perhaps the answer lies not just in what data we are able to detect but in what we are able to do with that information once it is ours to process.

To help conceptualize what I mean, consider the case of the heavenly bee. In heaven, this remarkable hymenopterous insect has been granted all the mentioned improvements. With its heightened senses and abilities, it can see a single flower from ten miles away and can smell the nectar from seven miles away. It can fly at incredible speed and can make more honey in a day than an earthly beehive could produce in a year.

There she goes now, zipping through the air at supersonic speed to a flower eight miles away and then back to the hive fully loaded with the treasure of incipient honey. All of this is impressive, but there are some things that the bee, still being a bee, is totally unaware of. She does not notice that there is an incredible sunrise taking place, and to get to that flower she just visited, she crossed over the Grand Canyon.

Though she has phenomenal hearing, she has no concept of music, and even if she may have been exposed at some point to Ferde Grofé's *Grand Canyon Suite*,[18] she has absolutely no inkling of the grandeur of the "Sunrise Movement." Thus, the heavenly bee fails to ascertain all but the minimal of what is there to be experienced and appreciated.

This would be like the experience that we would have, should we not be transmuted into beings capable of having a truly heavenly perspective. What sorts of underlying principles about the creation and what fundamental changes in us would govern our potential to fully realize what we are encountering? These are the background themes we will explore in Chapter 7.

CHAPTER 7

DISCOVERING THE UNIVERSAL TRUTHS

"For the foolishness of God is wiser than human wisdom,
and the weakness of God is stronger than human
strength."
1 CORINTHIANS 1:25

*Nothing exists except atoms and empty space; everything else is
opinion.*
DEMOCRITUS

A prudent question is one-half of wisdom.
FRANCIS BACON

*He who devotes sixteen hours a day to hard study may become at
sixty as wise as he thought himself at twenty.*
MARY WILSON LITTLE

At first glance our universe may seem to be a rather simple and ordinary place. From our perspective, things exist as solid or liquid, hot or cold, near or far, hard or soft, and so on.

Alas, this has much more to do with our limited capabilities of perception than with what is actually going on. It is the basis of—indeed the goal of— science to observe and explain our world and how and why it functions as it does. Having derived some concept of what is going on, the next task is to use this information and harness this new resource to some application and gain further knowledge. Humans have been about this task for several thousand years. Many of the finest minds in history have been devoted to this pursuit.

Ptolemy[1] used arithmetic calculations based on observation to predict future motions of planets and dates of eclipses. A video I once saw about Leonardo da Vinci[2] stated that as a child he observed ripples emanating from a point where a rock was tossed into pond and postulated the existence of sound waves. He also did studies of anatomy, mechanics, and flight.

Isaac Newton[3] co-invented a new branch of math called calculus, which he used to correct errors from the Ptolemaic model. Einstein[4] brought us the equivalence of matter and energy ($E = mc^2$). He told us that time is not a constant but is dependent on the motion of the observer and the observed and will be different (yet accurate) for each of them.

Even so, despite the brilliance of their combined efforts, we are still a long way from explaining the nature of what makes up this existence.

For any of you who had on your thinking caps when reading the chapter about the nature of time and the DVD, a thought may have occurred to you: I was told that *I was not in the movie but then appeared and finally was gone again. Well, that is true for my image, but the "real me" is not that image. The essential me is, in fact, the digital data that recorded on the disc that is projected by the player.*

You are correct, and in this analogy, that indelible piece of you on the disc correlates with that part of you called your soul. It may interest you to know that we are not the first ones to reach the conclusion that what we experience here may not be the ultimate reality. As a matter of fact, it was theorized several thousand years ago by Plato. He hypothesized about something that people today are trying to fathom using quantum mechanics.

The analogy of Plato's[5] cave appears as a portion of his work known as *The Republic.* [6] While generally regarded as a political treatise, to limit it to that realm would be to divorce the writing from Plato's perspective on life, that of the philosopher.[7]

"The contrast between ultimate reality and the world as it appears to the senses is of course familiar in philosophy and was already familiar in Plato's day. Parmenides had contrasted reality and appearance, and Plato's contemporary Democritus, from a very different point of view, regarded the world revealed by the senses as having only a secondary reality compared with the ultimate realities, atoms and void."[8]

The Republic is presented as a fictional conversation between Plato's brother, Glaucon, and Plato's teacher, Socrates. In this conversation, Socrates puts forth a scenario describing how people might be led to believe that what is in fact an illusion is itself reality. He describes a setting in which people have been imprisoned in a cave since they were old enough to begin forming memories.

They are chained in such a way that their arms, legs, and heads are immobile. Thus, they can only gaze at what is directly in front of them. Behind the prisoners is a raised walkway, and further back is an enormous, glowing fire.

When people pass over the walkway, their shadows are projected onto the wall monitored by the prisoners. Should those people be carrying objects, whatever shadow is cast is incorporated into their shadow on the wall. There is sound in the form of echoes from the walkway.

As the shadows and echoes are the only experience those in chains have ever known, they believe that both the shadows emanating from the real objects and the reflections from the real sounds are the reality itself.

In this scenario, there would likely be some people who would be more skilled at interpreting the shadows and sounds. They might be able to better guess what sound would be associated with a particular shadow, or what shadow might precede or follow another. They would likely be recognized by their fellow cave-dwellers as understanding "the true nature of the world." No one would conceive that what they were observing is not the real world at all. Nor would they grasp the actual nature of reality.

The argument considers the outcome should one of the prisoners be freed to experience the world and the difficulties he would encounter trying to explain his experience on returning to the cave.

You may be thinking, "Well, we certainly aren't in any cave. We know what reality is." If you think that you do know, let us consider just one facet of our existence, size. Just how big is big, and where would we fit in that scheme? I encourage you to guess just where you measure up to the rest of the universe.

When we speak of size, we need to utilize some defined increment of measure. Instead, of using linguistic terms like "nano", which when added to meter (nanometer) means one billionth of a meter, let us use scientific notation, a simple concept where the addition or subtraction of a zero from in front of or behind a number denotes a change of tenfold. For example, $10^0 = 1$, $10^1 = 10$, $10^2 = 100$, $10^3 = 1000$. Conversely, $10^{-1} = 0.1$, $10^{-2} = 0.01$, $10^{-3} = 0.001$ and so on. Thus, we can consider that small number (called superscript) appearing above and behind the main number as the number of zeros either before (in the case of negative superscript) or after (in the case of positive superscript) the "1". By example, most humans are between 1.5 and 1.8 meters tall or 1.5 to 1.8 x 10^0 meters tall. I will say an average of about 1.6 meters. A soccer field is about 100 or 10^2 meters in length. Using this format, a lightyear (the distance light will travel at 186,000 miles per second over the course of a year) is 5,879,000,000,000,000 or 5.879 x 10^{12} miles which converts to 9.46 x 10^{15} meters. The observable (27.4 billion light years) **plus** the currently unobservable universe, is thought to **total** approximately 93 billion light years or 8.8 x 10^{26} meters in diameter. Wow, at 1.6 meters I feel exceptionally small and lost in the universe right about now. 10^{-2} meters is called a centimeter or 1/100 meter and is about the width of your thumb nail.

My second suggestion would be that on the "small end", to continue to shrink until what is accepted as being the smallest length attainable in this universe (called a Planck length) is reached. This value was derived by German theoretical physicist Max Planck, by utilizing three constants: the speed of light in a vacuum, Newton's gravitational constant, and Planck's constant. It is calculated as being 1.6 x 10^{-35} meters. Just how small is that? Let's start with an atom. Atoms are about 100,000 times smaller than we can see without magnification. Imagine that you are in a spacecraft orbiting the earth. As you gaze down you are looking for the smallest structure that you can see with your unaided vision. There is a tiny red dot in the middle of the Sahara Desert. That dot is a sphere with a diameter of about 7 miles. An atom in comparison to that sphere would be the size of a softball. Next, we compare a Planck length to that atom. If we want to construct a line of Planck lengths to span the diameter of that atom laying them "end to end" at a rate of one Planck length per second, it will take 4.352×10^{24} seconds or about **10,000,000 times** the current age of the universe **(10^7 x 13.8 billion** years **x 365** day/year **x 24** hours/day **x 60** minutes/hour **x 60** seconds/minute) to accomplish our goal. Now that is tiny!

In all the size variation of the universe, where do we fit in? In going from the biggest to smallest we see that we have a difference of 62 orders of magnitude (10^{26} to 10^{-35}). That is, there has been a size change of 10-fold that has occurred 62 times over. Thus, changing by 31 orders of magnitude from either end will put us halfway on the scale. Thus, adding 31 orders of magnitude to the small end of -35 yields a midpoint of 10^{-4} meters. So, at 1.6 meters height we are still 10,000 times larger than the midpoint! Give yourself a high five! God has made a big deal of you! He is God of the universe and Planck lengths. Hopefully your idea of what reality consists of has taken a jolt.

Why do I bring this up? We are all familiar with the four dimensions through which we navigate: height, width, depth, and time. But suppose I told you that there could be at least seven other dimensions in existence that we do not personally experience.[9] Would you think me daft or given to flights of fancy?

That there are dimensions in existence beyond what we know experientially should not come as any surprise to us as Christians. Are we not told that "war broke out in heaven" (Revelation 12:7) and "for in him all things were created: things in heaven and on earth, visible and invisible" (Colossians 1:16)? If our souls survive our own physical death, they must exist in something other than what we currently experience. Indeed, we should champion poly-dimensionality, because without it our core beliefs would not be possible.

Quantum mechanics is a powerful mathematical tool dedicated to plumbing the reaches of the hidden realm of the fundamental properties of energy. It has helped scientists make predictions that have led to such marvelous inventions as the cell phone and the plasma television. It deals directly with the behavior of existence in the sub, sub, sub-atomic world and how that dictates what we see on the grandest of all scales, the visible universe. It also has pushed astrophysicists to consider the possibility of concepts like string theory,[10] superstrings[11] and super symmetry.[12] Extra dimensions are required for at least the latter two.

Quantum physics was first introduced as a study in 1900 when Max Planck[13] proposed the concept that electromagnetic energy is composed of discrete packets called quanta. The underlying theory holds that the universe sprang from a solitary form of energy. If you were trying to explain this concept to someone who did not have any scientific background, you might say something catchy yet concise like, "Let there be light."

If we could combine Einstein's general relativity describing the large scale of the universe with quantum mechanics to describe the ultramicroscopic aspects of existence, we would have the best tool for exploring how everything in the universe is derived from that energy. As I mentioned earlier, Einstein brought us an equation by which we can equate mass and energy and show that the two are the same, differing only in form.

Another brilliant man named James Clerk Maxwell[14] derived equations to describe a concept first put forth by Michael Faraday,[15] showing that electrical energy and magnetism were likewise equivalent—though different — manifestations of the same thing.

Another of the fundamental forces of the laws of physics is termed the weak nuclear force. This force operates just within the nucleus itself and governs radioactive decay and dictates much about how fusion itself happens.[16] In the 1970s theorists were successful in combining it with electro-magnetism, again showing a type of equivalence and dubbing it the electroweak force.

The strong nuclear force is that force that allows for the formation of atoms with more than one proton. That is, it allows for the formulation of the elements beyond hydrogen. Without this force, the protons (each having a positive charge) would repel each other whenever they came in proximity.[17]

If we were able to combine this force with the electroweak force, we would have achieved what is called a grand unified theory. Thus far this has not been possible. The theory of gravitational force (possibly gravitons) has been the other outlier as far as integrating it with the other forms of energy. Unifying all of the forces results in what is called the theory of everything. I prefer to call it God's big theory of everything, or God's big TOE.

The theory states that everything must derive from the one source, and that includes gravity, all matter (including dark matter), all energy (including dark energy), time, and empty space itself. That means they are all a latent manifestation of that primal energy. Therefore, there should be an equivalency factor for converting energy into gravitational force.

Energy manifesting itself as "empty space" is even more complicated than it sounds. A close acquaintance who speaks the dialect of mathematics fluently puts it like this: "If you mean the vacuum, note that by Heisenberg's uncertainty principle, particles of any kind can emerge from the vacuum so long as they remerge back into the vacuum before the time uncertainty has elapsed. As one physicist put it, 'The vacuum is a plenum.'"[18] Or, as I think I understand it, empty space is not actually empty. Let us give some further consideration to that vacuum. It turns out that the energy, which I take to be that force necessary to create and maintain "empty" dimensionality, sometimes called vacuum energy or zero-point energy, is enormous. In fact, it has been calculated that if one was able to release the energy in a mayonnaise jar size vacuum, it could boil off the earth's oceans in 3 seconds! That this energy could and would continue to have the capability of changing form, as it did in the creation scenario, should come as no big surprise to us. The ultimate dream of quantum theory is to be able to derive formulae that show how every manifestation of our physical universe can be derived from one primal form of energy.

The fact that there are equations showing the relationships between mass, energy, electricity, and magnetism, weak nuclear force, and electromagnetism (and likely other formulae unifying the remaining forces) is testament to the fact that the universe is not random but is exquisitely and precisely put together and complex in its functions. Just how precisely?

"First, the mean density of matter in the universe at the very beginning has to be within 1 part in 10^{60} of the so-called 'critical density' which demarcates universes which are open (expand forever) from those that are closed (re-collapse to a 'big crunch'). If the density is smaller than it is by this amount, then the universe will expand too quickly for the galaxies and stars to be able to form. If it is greater, then the whole universe will re-collapse under the gravity in just a few months. Either way you have a boring universe with no possibility of life. An accuracy of 1 part in 10^{60} is that required to aim a gun at a coin 14 billion light-years away at the opposite end of the universe and hit it!"[19] There are approximately 80 other similar requirements for precision that go into making our universe a functional place in which to exist. Another astrophysicist put it this way. The odds of this universe existing by chance are about the same as those of taking a butterfly net, making one blind swipe and capturing the ONE red electron in this universe.

What are the implications? Imagine this. You are on a game show called Let's Make A Deal. Monty Hall (look him up if you don't know who he was) is interviewing you. You are putting not just what you've accrued on his show, but also your entire life savings on the line. If you pick correctly, you need never worry again about your ability to have all that you desire. If you are in error, there awaits unremitting poverty and want. There are two doors (not three as in the TV show) to choose from and you MUST play, you MUST pick one of them. Door number one is labeled, "There is no God." Door number two is labeled, "God exists". Monty points to door number one and says, "The chances of this being the correct door to choose are the same as the odds of finding that one red electron in the universe." He then gestures toward door number two. "I can't prove to you that this is a better choice," he states, "but I can assure you that the odds are greater than zero AND if you pick door one, you are in effect stating that you believe the chances of door number two being correct are LESS than the odds I quoted to you for door number one. Additionally, ONE of the two IS the CORRECT answer." What rational choice would you make? As for me, "Hey Monty, give me door number TWO!"

I once heard a very well-known astrophysicist state that perhaps the universe resulted from "a quantum fluctuation", essentially accepting door number one as his choice. In doing so, it is posited that our universe, among infinitely many multiverses (there is no proof of any other universes), happened to be the one that beat the odds above. I do understand that scientists have an obligation to try to explain things on a rational level rather than attributing it to God without further investigation. Yet, I believe that there is a point when denial of evidence for God becomes irrational. Let's again look at the astrophysicist contention about creation being a matter of "quantum fluctuation".

I see three major problems that I do not think that he considered. The first is that since these fluctuations happen in the realm of empty space, how could one occur when there is NO space, i.e., no dimensionality, which is the "pre-creation" condition? Second, he seems to have lapsed in not considering that time itself is a construct of this universe, that is, a result of that energy and would not have come into being without the primal energy. If time does not exist, then I see no reasonable way for a "fluctuation" – which implies change over time, to occur. Finally, quantum fluctuation in what exactly? Since he is discussing the appearance and disappearance of particles, and we know that matter and energy are equivalent from $E=mc^2$, we must assume that he is referring to quantum fluctuation in the energy present. However, since that primal energy does not exist until creation, there exists nothing to have fluctuation in. Thus, quantum fluctuation likewise seems intrinsic to this universe. If he then resorts to a "pre-existent" space and /or time and/or energy, then we are right back to square one in having something that we have no proof of and no scientific explanation for.

"But God chose the foolish things of the world to shame the wise; God chose the weak things of the world to shame the strong. God chose the lowly things of this world and the despised things—and the things that are not—to nullify the things that are, so that no one may boast before him" (1 Corinthians 1:27–29).

Albert Einstein, Max Planck, and Edwin Hubble. Many of us are at least familiar with these names, who are some of the finest minds and Nobel laureates in science. But probably most of you are not familiar with names like Leslie Lemke, Kim Peek, or Alonzo Clemons. These individuals and others like them impress me as being evidence from the other extreme of the intellectual spectrum of basic, immutable truths that permeate the universe and the nature of existence. I refer to the spectacle of what is known as savant syndrome.

This phenomenon was first described in 1887 by John Langdon Down, who also documented the characteristics of what later came to be called Down syndrome.[20] He described savantism as a condition in which some individuals with developmental brain abnormality—otherwise regarded as retarded in their capacities—might show profound abilities within a very limited spectrum. Originally this was known as *idiot savant* (from the French meaning "learned idiot") syndrome.

I do not know if the subjects he studied truly fit the medical definition of the term *idiot* (IQ of less than 25),[21] or if he was using it more generically for someone of less than average intelligence. In any case, the term is outmoded, as many savants have IQs well more than that and approaching normalcy. The most common aberrancy of development associated with savantism is autism. It is said that up to 1 in 10 autistic people may manifest some unusual abilities and around 50 percent of savants are autistic.[22]

These individuals, though generally thought of as handicapped, have been given a special insight into a very limited width (but profoundly deep) slice of some portion of a basic tenet on which reality is founded. Some of these capabilities we can somewhat relate to, like a musical talent or prodigious feat of memory. Some savants may manifest exemplary artistic skill, such as the ability to sculpt or paint in accurate detail after only a momentary glance at a subject.

Some have abilities that seem to make no sense to us at all. A savant may be able to state the day of the week associated with any date—even to several thousand years in the past or future and accounting for leap years— but be devoid of any mathematical skills to the point they cannot do even the most basic addition.

While there have been a many people who have been classified as musically gifted savants, the first one I remember hearing about, and the only one I have ever witnessed in person, is a man named Leslie Lemke. Leslie was born in Milwaukee, Wisconsin, in 1952. He was born premature and noted to have brain damage early on, even lacking a sucking reflex. Because of the development of glaucoma, his eyes were surgically removed before he was six months of age.

He was destined to have a profound form of cerebral palsy. With the infant given up for adoption by his parents, a hospital official made a call to a former nurse who had raised five children of her own and asked if she would take him under her care until his imminent death. She agreed to take the child but vowed that he would not die.

May Lemke would take small amounts of food and gently place it into and push it down the back of his throat to sustain him. She placed a pacifier in his mouth and then made sucking noises with her own mouth near his ear so that he might respond in kind. In this way, she was able to teach him to suck. By about the time he was a year old, he had learned this skill and then was able to feed with a bottle. The following year he was able to chew his food.

Leslie never made a sound and did not spontaneously move. Mrs. Lemke would spend hours holding him, singing to him, praying for him. He could not sit up by himself and had to be tied into a chair. By the time he was eight years old and still could not stand, Mrs. Lemke and her husband rigged a way to bind Leslie to her with his arms around her waist.

For the next three years she would take him out in the yard and walk around, dragging him behind. Her husband would take him down to the nearby lake in the summer and move him up and down in the water in hopes of stimulating some standing response. When he was 11, they put in chain-link fence for the purpose of teaching him to stand. She would prop him up against this. At age 12 he finally pulled himself up to a standing position. It would be another three years before he finally started to walk.

Mrs. Lemke frequently had music on in the house, though Leslie showed no signs of listening.[23] At one point, she noted that he was plucking on a string, and it occurred to her that perhaps he liked music. She and her husband bought a $250 piano. She would take Leslie and either press some of the keys down or press his fingers down on, individual notes.

Then one night, when Leslie was about 16 years old, the family had watched (Leslie obviously didn't) and heard (Leslie did) a movie on television. May Lemke awoke around 3 a.m. the next morning to the sound of music in the dark house. She woke her husband to ask if he had left the television on, and he said he had not.

As she walked through the unlit house, she discovered the sound was not coming from the living room but from the bedroom where they kept the piano. In that dimly lit room, she witnessed what would be classified in anyone's terms a miracle. There was Leslie, who struggled to feed himself (and as far as I know, never could use utensils because he could not hold them), sitting at the piano perfectly playing the theme music to the movie they had all heard. It was Tchaikovsky's Piano Concerto no. 1.[24, 25]

Within about a year after starting to play, Leslie began to sing, and within another year sang confidently, his voice intoning whoever he had heard render the tune, from Louis Armstrong to Al Jolson. It would be another eight years before he began to talk. Once Leslie hears a tune, it apparently stays in his repertoire indefinitely.

There is more to the story, and I invite the reader to watch video of his story and performances.

For those of you who occasionally see movies, you may remember a scene that, as I understand it, was based on a real incident, in the movie *Rain Man*.[26] In this portion of the movie a box of toothpicks is knocked to the floor and the savant, played by Dustin Hoffman,[27] glances down at the tangle of toothpicks and says, "82, 82, 82." To which another character responds that there a lot more than 82 toothpicks in the pile, failing to comprehend that the savant sees the jumble as consisting of three distinct piles of 82 objects each. The total of 246 toothpicks spilled is later verified. The person who Hoffman spent time within order to learn how a savant might act was Kim Peek.

Peek was born in 1951. He had developmental delays, including not being able to walk until the age of four. Part of this may have been due to some congenital brain abnormality in which the two halves of the brain are missing their main connection with each other, what is called the corpus callosum. This made for at least one interesting ability: being able to read two pages of a book at the same time; one page with each eye.[28]

Like the savant portrayed in the movie, Peek had a prodigious memory with information about music dates, geography, and other areas. (I don't know about airline crash statistics but would not doubt he knew them as well.) He could concisely recall the content of at least 12,000 books from memory, despite having a somewhat less than average IQ of 87 (average is 100).[29] As with Lemke, there is more to his story to explore as the reader sees fit.

For my final example of phenomenal abilities, I refer to Daniel Tammet. This young man carries the diagnosis of autism and had recurrent seizures as a young child. He is highly functional, especially in the realm of languages and mathematics. At the time of my research, he reportedly spoke eleven languages. One of these is Icelandic, a difficult language to master. He became fluent in it within one week.

He came into the public eye while raising money for the National Society for Epilepsy by reciting pi from memory to 22,514 decimal places.[30] What fascinates me the most about this young man is the following: "Numbers, according to Daniel, are special to him. He has a rare form of synesthesia and sees each integer up to 10,000 as having their own unique shapes, color, texture, and feel. He can 'see' the result of a math calculation, and he can 'sense' whether a number is prime. Daniel has since drawn what pi looks like: a rolling landscape full of different shapes and colors."[31]

In other words, Tammet does not calculate the answer to a math problem; he intuitively senses it. It is a thing of beauty to him—a perfect piece needed to complete a puzzle.

What these special people do seems impossible. That they do have these gifts is only possible if there are the underpinnings of truth there to begin with. Chaos does not account for these abilities. Randomness does not strike with such profound accuracy.

There are ways of perceiving the universe that are beyond our ability to even guess from our current vantage point. It has long been my contention that we all suffer from what I would term a relative dysgnostia. By that I mean that we all have varying degrees of lack of insight into the fundamentals of reality. In some areas we may have less intuitive grasp than our friend or neighbor. In other fields, we may have more. However, no one on this planet, no matter how brilliant, has full insight into it all.

It seems inescapable to me that when all the evidence is looked at, there are indeed underlying, basic, and immutable truths to the way that the universe functions. To those who are willing to totally ascribe this to any degree of sheer chance, I say, "Poppycock, fiddlesticks, and balderdash." (I could have used a more concise term that starts with the word "bull" but my wife thought it inappropriate.) To attribute these qualities to creation without causation takes a far greater leap of faith in "chance" than does a realization of the likelihood of a creator, i.e., God.

Now let us imagine that in addition to the enhanced senses we discussed in Chapter 6, we have now been granted the type of insight into these immutable truths that the savants seem to possess. But it is combined with an intellect far beyond what anyone on this earth is capable of having.

It is as if that heavenly bee is suddenly capable not only of hearing and appreciating music in a way that Beethoven never could have but is herself also able to compose far greater music. She has the capacity to not only take in the spectacle of the Grand Canyon but also notes the patterns on the rocks and the stories they tell. She sees the light of the sun and intuitively understands entirely how it can act as both a particle and a wave at the same time—something we don't currently understand.

The bee now fully comprehends the magic and magnificence of the creation with which it is surrounded. This is analogous to what we are destined for in the realm of heaven. To say that it will be "mind blowing" or "astounding" is only a testament to my lack of better vocabulary.

Even so, everything we have thus far encountered lies at the periphery of our heavenly experience and does not ultimately solve the riddle of tedium with respect to eternity. For our best chance to realize never-ending contentment, we must look to the core of heaven and there find God Himself and what He intends for us. These notions are contemplated in the final two chapters.

CHAPTER 8

MAKING LIGHT OF GOD

Let the light of your face shine on us.
PSALM 4:6

My God turns my darkness into light.
PSALM 18:28

The LORD is my light and my salvation—whom shall I fear?
PSALM 27:1

The LORD wraps himself in light as with a garment.
PSALM 104:2

For the LORD will be your everlasting light.
ISAIAH 60:19

I am the light of the world.
Whoever follows me will never walk in darkness,
but will have the light of life.
JOHN 8:12

It is better to light a candle than to curse the darkness.
ELEANOR ROOSEVELT

*Faith is the strength by which a shattered world shall emerge
into the light.*
HELEN KELLER

*We can easily forgive a child who is afraid of the dark; the real
tragedy of life is when men are afraid of the light.*

PLATO

I am impressed by the number of times the word *light* is used in the Bible. What's more, it is frequently used as a defining quality of the nature of God. I do not believe this is at all by accident or happenstance. I do not think that it is the result of faulty translation from one language to another. I am confident that it is intentionally placed there by God's will that we should note and consider it deeply.

It is important to think of this light not just as that portion of the electromagnetic spectrum I discussed earlier, but to understand it as the truth that is the Spirit of God. I also think that, when we consider the implications of this light, it can give us another level of understanding, or at least another way to look at God's nature as well as our nature and how, without some type of intermediary, we, as we currently are, cannot exist in His presence.

If any of you have any casual acquaintance with astrophysics or have even gone to the occasional science-fiction movie, you may have heard the term *neutrino*. The neutrino, it turns out, is not just a figment of a sci-fi writer's imagination; it does exist. A facility at the South Pole designated in the scientific community as the Ice Cube Neutrino Observatory[1] consists of 86 holes spread out over a 1kilometer square surface area. Each hole is drilled to a depth of 1.2 miles.

Into each hole are lowered optical sensors on a cable to a depth of between 4,757 and 8,038 feet. At these depths, the ice is exceedingly clear and dark. The sole purpose of this facility is to measure the neutrinos' interaction with more conventional (but likewise invisible to us) particles that we are more familiar with, the hydrogen atom.

It turns out that the neutrino is named so because it has neither a positive nor a negative charge and is thus neutral. It is of exceedingly small mass on the order of 3.2×10^{-39} ounces (0.0000 0000000000000000000000000000000032 ounces), roughly 1 million times less massive than a single electron.[2]

I know that still doesn't register, does it? Let me put it this way: Let's enlarge the neutrino to something that we could see, say a grain of sand. If we take that grain of sand and multiply it by a factor of 10^{39}, we end up with 1×10^{39} grains. That amount of sand would be enough to construct about 3,000 earths or a sphere with about twice the volume of Jupiter.

Compare the size difference between our original grain of sand and this giant sphere. Now, we take that very large sphere and shrink it down to the size of a ping-pong ball filled with sand. Then if we take our original grain of sand and shrink it down by a commensurate amount, we end up with something about the size of a neutrino. But whether we are talking grains, ounces, or years, I think that some way of visualizing these ridiculously large or small numbers helps us to understand.

These phantom neutrinos are produced in the core of the sun by its ongoing nuclear reaction, and every second billions of them pass through every one of our bodies. If that is the case, then why don't we feel them, or why don't they harm us? It turns out that the properties mentioned above give the neutrino some interesting capabilities, not the least of which is the ability to pass seemingly effortlessly through matter without ever interacting with it. How profound is this ability?

It is said that for a neutrino to have a chance of greater than 50 percent of striking an atom of lead (a dense material that, as I am sure most of you are aware, even Superman[3] could not see through!), the sheet of lead would have to be one light-year thick.[4]

What is a light-year? It's like a regular year with half of the calories. (No, excuse me, I was thinking of a lite beer.) A light-year is the distance that light will travel in one year. At 186,000 miles per second, times 60 seconds per minute, times 60 minutes per hour, times 24 hours per day, times 365 days, it works out to about 6 trillion (6,000,000,000,000 or 6×10^{12}) miles.

Earth is only eight light-minutes from the sun. So, as you can see, that would be a most prodigious sheet of lead. So why the long discourse on neutrinos? I propose that we can think of God's transmitted glory (Spirit) as analogous to having the penetrating power of a neutrino.

However, unlike the neutrino, the Spirit will destroy anything it encounters that is contrary to its nature. Think of it this way: If you were a light bulb, what would you see? You would not see any shadow because you yourself are the source of the light, and any shadow is driven away by your view.

Now, there are obviously shadows when we turn on a light, but like the neutrino, God's Spirit is not hindered by any object.

I further contend that to come into His kingdom and appear before Him will be to come forever into the full presence of that Holy Spirit.

In my bathroom I have a couple of special light fixtures. The bulbs that fit in these lamps are 50-watt halogen devices. Though they are only about the size of a man's index finger from second knuckle to tip (approximately two inches), they provide much greater illumination than standard incandescent bulbs.

The literature that comes with the bulbs warns against touching them with bare skin and advises using gloves to replace them.

Of course, it would be foolish to touch that surface if the light had just been on, but the instructions implicitly state "never." The instructions further state that any touching "may reduce the life expectancy of the lamp." Why is this? Because any residue of dirt or oil from the skin will result in the glass at that spot absorbing more of the radiant energy and converting it to heat. That heat is not only harder on the internal component of the light, but it could also shatter the glass. To maximize the life expectancy of the bulb, it must be as transparent to the energy going through it as possible.

Now let us consider our nature. Have any of you ever wanted to go on a vacation and leave all your cares behind? You planned, you waited, and you executed your plan, but to your dismay, once you arrived at your destination, you found that the one person you most wanted to leave behind had joined you on the trip. (No, I am not speaking of your mother-in-law.) I am speaking of you, the imperfect you who always brings the worries, the stresses—and worst—the truth about your nature.

All but the most non-self-aware of us knows we are not perfect—far from it. We are all too cognizant of our shortcomings: our temper, jealousy, envy, lust, anxiety, depression, guilt, doubt, fear, loneliness, and grief. All these character flaws originate and thrive in the realm of darkness. Until you have been a slave to them you cannot really appreciate how each is a cruel and unrelenting task master, inflicting its own unique brand of torture.

We are also prone to error in ways that may make us transiently feel good about ourselves. If we are self-righteous, then we feel superior and perhaps somehow feel justified in using others to fulfill our perceived needs.

We have all had times when we have given in to those baser emotions and fallen short of what we know to be the right thing to do.

In Christianity, this inherent predisposition to fall short of the ideal is termed the sin nature. Perhaps Britney Spears[5] may have referred to it in a different way in a pop song called "Oops!...I Did It Again."[6] We know that the Apostle Paul was all too familiar with his spiritual flaws. In Romans 7:22–24 we read, "For in my inner being I delight in God's law; but I see another law at work in me, waging war against the law of my mind and making me a prisoner of the law of sin at work within me. What a wretched man I am!"

One of the great purposes of the Old Testament was to make us aware of the presence of this nature in all our lives. Psalm 14:1 puts it this way: "They are corrupt, their deeds are vile; there is no one who does good." It turns out that this sin nature puts spots on us much as any soiling does on those halogen bulbs. If 110 volts will destroy a slightly dirtied light, imagine the degree of "cleanness" one would have to possess in order to come into the energy field of a power so great that it could create a universe simply by speaking it into existence!

This imperfect nature is incapable of existing in the full presence of God and communing with Him without destroying its vessel, which I will call the soul. In fact, to come into proximity with God while bearing this burden is to realize utter destruction. One would have a better chance of surviving a walk on the surface of the sun than of standing before God in our flawed state.

Exodus 33:20 gives us God's own testimony to this effect. Moses has just asked to see the glory of God and the Lord replies, "You cannot see my face, for no one may see me and live." This is the reason we can never hope to reach to God based on our own merit.

Galatians 3:10 states it this way: "For all who rely on the works of the law are under a curse, as it is written: 'Cursed is everyone who does not continue to do everything written in the Book of the Law.'" That first time any of us ever made the slightest departure from perfection of spirit was fatal to us.

The Old Testament provides a striking example of this in the opening sentences of Leviticus chapter 10: "Aaron's sons Nadab and Abihu took their censers, put fire in them and added incense; and they offered unauthorized fire before the LORD, contrary to his command. So, fire came out from the presence of the LORD and consumed them, and they died before the LORD."

At first glance, you may think this to be some petty act of God, but that is only because you have failed to grasp the holiness of God. I would argue that what happened to them was the inevitable consequence of their action, much as if they had stepped off a high cliff and fallen under the force of gravity to their deaths. The difference between gravity and God's holiness is that His holiness is more certain.

I think that there are two central truths that separate Christianity's concept of God from other notions of God. The first is His absolute and unapproachable holiness. As I hope to show, I do not think God took any delight in the demise of Nadab and Abihu and, in fact, was grieved by it. Ezekiel 18:32 says, "For I take no pleasure in the death of anyone, declares the Sovereign LORD. Repent and live!" Similarly, Paul notes in 1 Timothy 2:3-4 that "God our Savior, who wants all people to be saved and to come to a knowledge of the truth."

We each have a major problem. Like the light bulb, we are inescapably incapable of removing any smudges from ourselves or others. Performing an act of sacrifice or kindness cannot erase our less-than-perfect moments. Our "good works" are only those things we should have done in the first place to maintain a right relationship with God.

As Jesus stated in Luke 17:10, "So you also, when you have done everything you were told to do, should say, 'We are unworthy servants; we have only done our duty.'" When perfection is the minimum acceptable standard, there is no way to go but down. Then what hope does any of us have? Can there be any other outcome but doom?

Thankfully, it is not up to us to provide a solution to our dilemma. As incredible as it sounds, the One who created all and set the foundations for how and why the universe works, loves you, the reader of this book. If you ask why, you will be in excellent company. As the psalmist wrote, "When I consider your heavens, the work of your fingers, the moon and the stars, which you have set in place, what is mankind that you are mindful of them, human beings that you care for them?" (Psalm 8:3–4)

At this juncture it is worthwhile to consider the perfect nature of God and what implications this has when we consider what it means to be "forgiven" by God.

My spouse, or my child, sibling, friend, or neighbor may forgive me for some transgression out of the "goodness of their heart," or perhaps because they have experienced what it is to be forgiven. This type of forgiveness is tantamount to a conscious decision to override the natural proclivity of feeling a need for repayment or revenge. Actual payment for the wrong suffered may not be required, although a sincere "I am sorry" can certainly aid in the healing. However, because of His nature, God does not have this simple option. Some might argue that God can do "anything". This is easily disproved. For example, God can not sin. It is not in His nature. And in the same way, it is also impossible for Him to simply forgive without the offences being paid for.

Though many will try to blame God for all sorts of wrongs they may have witnessed or suffered, He has performed no wrongs. Therefore, He cannot be the grateful recipient of any forgiveness. Some may cite some natural disaster like an earthquake or tornado or some machination of man like war or tribal genocide as "proof" that God does wrong. They miss the larger picture. God does allow things to happen—things that are in contradiction to His best will.

Without this simple truth, you and I could not experience what it is to have free will. And this world and nature suffer from being out of communion with Him. But God's goodness and His power are such that He can take these circumstances and ultimately use them to accomplish the best possible result.

Because we lack God's perspective on just what this will entail, He has acknowledged that we will not always see "eye to eye" with Him about what is best at any given moment. As stated in Isaiah 55:9, "As the heavens are higher than the earth, so are my ways higher than your ways and my thoughts than your thoughts."

On occasion I have stumbled on a nugget of good theology in an unexpected source. I remember a deleted scene from the 2003 movie *Bruce Almighty* in which God (played by Morgan Freeman) is discussing with Bruce (Jim Carrey) the wisdom in not granting some prayer requests immediately in order to achieve a greater good in the long term. As I recall, the specifics dealt with Bruce having granted the prayer of a woman to be rescued from bankruptcy. I would think that to most of us this appears to be a very worthwhile request. In the short term, she became rich, but because of her financial independence, she missed out on an opportunity she would have had to reconnect with her long-estranged sister, an outcome that God deemed more valuable.

The greatest example of wisdom I can think of in this regard comes from scripture itself. God allowed His greatest enemy, Satan, to act in free will and perform the ultimate feat of hate and vileness in orchestrating the murder of God's innocent Son. Lucifer's showpiece pinnacle of power was to kill God incarnate—a move calculated to presumably prohibit the divine from influencing man and thereby ensure our enslavement to him. God's unprecedented response is to use that very act to accomplish the Devil's defeat and bring about the greatest possible good: glorification of His Son and the salvation of our souls.

While I suspect few would argue that God lacks "goodness of heart," His nature does not allow a simple mental assent on His part to forgive sin. He absolutely cannot tolerate sin, that is, sin cannot exist in His presence.

Therefore, that sin must be atoned for in full. Galatians 2:20 says, "I have been crucified with Christ and I no longer live, but Christ lives in me. The life I now live in the body, I live by faith in the Son of God, who loved me and gave himself for me." The direct implication is that God's forgiveness has taken the form of a transference of our sin debt from us and onto His Son.

We humans are incapable of surviving any attempt to pay for our own sin. "For the wages of sin is death," (our souls simply could not survive the process) "but the gift of God is eternal life in Christ Jesus our Lord" (Romans 6:23). This is why Acts 4:12 states, "Salvation is found in no one else, for there is no other name under heaven given to mankind by which we must be saved." And Jesus himself stated, "I am the way and the truth and the life. No one comes to the Father except through me" (John 14:6).

Perhaps it was my Catholic upbringing, or perhaps it was just watching Charlton Heston[7] in too many biblical epics, but until recently I have had a concept of God as being distinctly separated and not terribly interested in my life. Beyond that, He had a long white beard and was carrying a big stick, just waiting—in fact eagerly anticipating—for me to step out of line so He could give me a good whack!

I am sure I was told differently than that, but it is one thing to assent to a mental concept and quite another to feel it in one's heart. I think it was this flawed perception more than anything else that led me to reject Christianity carte blanche in my mid to later teen years. Even after, as an adult, I came to believe in Jesus as God's Son and my Savior, my view of God the Father was that of austerity.

It is only after much pondering that I have concluded that God is, in contradistinction to that presupposition, desperate to have a relationship with us. "God desperate?" you say. "This does not fit with my concept of God, floating serenely above the clouds, all wise and all powerful. How could God possibly be described as desperate?"

You may be correct in taking exception to this term but only because "desperate" is not severe enough to describe the situation. How desperate to achieve your goal would you have to be to send your only son to another place, for the first time away from you, knowing that he would be given over to your sworn enemy, severely mistreated, tortured, and murdered?

Worse, all the tarnish that we had accumulated on ourselves— all that makes it impossible to stand before God without being utterly destroyed— was to be transmitted to your beloved son, as he was assigned to bear the consequence for us. Imagine how much Jesus loved the Father and us. He had been in intimate relationship with God always, and he would now be totally shut out of that presence.

If God is life and light, then to be utterly excluded from Him is indeed to experience death and ultimate darkness. We can never hope to really grasp all that this exclusion implies. Suffice it to say that no mortal being could endure it and live. That is why God chose to send the only one who could.

Would you be willing to sacrifice your own son or daughter in this way? Would you love your own father enough to volunteer?

What was borne on the cross was much deeper and more profound than anything witnessed by the humans who were present. What happens to an immortal being when he is subjected to death? In our experience, darkness is always subject to light. That is, if a place is dark and then one turns on a light, the darkness flees. But this is as if you could go into a light place and "turn on the dark," making the light flee.

All of this was just to make it possible for you and me to be able to finally come to Him, from the outer darkness and into His light. Can there be any other remedy? If there were any way for us to reach up to God on our own, would He have extracted such a heavy toll on Himself and His Son as to go through that literal hell? Could there be any greater definition of love? I am convinced not. This is the second foundational truth that separates Christianity's God from any other: the unfathomable depth of His love for us.

On judgment day, those who have refused to accept this provision will have to give account of why. I am afraid they will not have a sufficient answer. Those of us who have accepted this truth will be asked a similar if not quite as damning question: "Knowing what you did about Me, why did you act the way you did, think and say the things you did, and not share in word and deed, the Truth about Me that you knew could have saved those who now stand condemned in My presence?" I really don't want to have to come up with an answer for that one either. Is this a portion of my motivation for writing this book? Quite possibly.

"God hates sin." This sounds more than a little pejorative at first as if God has decided to take exception with something just because He decided He wanted to. Nothing could be further from the truth. Given the above, how would you feel about something that, without the remedy cited above, was going to take your loved ones forever away from you and condemn them to the darkest pit of misery? How would you state your enmity for something so foul as to cause you to pay such a horrific price?

For me, the central mystery of Christianity is twofold. First, why would God possibly love us that much? Second, how was Jesus able to take away our stain?

I will deal with the second question before contemplating the first. It says in Galatians 2:20 that we have been "crucified with Christ." What does that mean?

As my oldest son has endeavored to educate me, there have been a variety of atonement theories put forth down through the ages. First is the ransom theory. This states that we are rightfully the property of the enemy (Satan) due to our sin. God, because of His nature, cannot enter these realms to rescue His captive people. That is, should He come fully into that place, it would destroy the place and the captives He wishes to free. The incarnation is thus a great infiltration of humanity with God's divinity. The crucifixion is the cosmic fishhook with Christ's flesh as the bait and His divinity as the hook. The resurrection is the destruction of the devil's greatest weapon—death—and the rescue of those souls willing to accept His provision for them.

Then there is the penal substitution theory. This is attributed largely to Anselm of Canterbury[8] from around 1070. It involves "the great chain of being," which stretches from God down to man. Sin acts to disrupt the set order by causing a breach of honor. The importance of the offense depends on the rank of the offended and not the offender. Any offense must be compensated for by a corresponding restoration of honor. In this case, since the offense is against an infinitely supreme entity, it must be paid for with an infinite penalty. That being the case, only God is capable of paying the penalty.

Peter Abelard[9] (1079–1142) proposed the moral influence theory. This model rejected traditional concepts like original sin, vicarious atonement, and sin as a force. It asserted that God is love and could not show wrath either to us or to Jesus. Therefore, God, of His own free will and abundant grace, had already forgiven sins before Christ even died. Christ's sacrifice was simply the ultimate expression of true love: a willingness to die for an undeserving beloved.

Finally comes the theory of Christ the perfect penitent. We are made in God's image and likeness. We still retain a semblance of that image, but it became tarnished at the fall. Christ assumed our fallenness at His incarnation. Through Christ's sacrifice, we are able to attain His nature by His work within us. Christ is the bond and meeting point: because He is man, He is one with us; because He is God, He is one with the Father. So, through Him and in Him we are one with God.

One can make arguments for and against each one of these theories and, since I have no theological training, I am the least qualified to give any kind of exegetical dissertation on them. Having said that, there is a saying about the Thomas clan that I first heard from another Thomas: "You can always tell a Thomas, but you can't tell 'em much." Thus, as author, I will assert my prerogative and state that I do find certain aspects of these stratagems very thought provoking.

However, I still find them unsatisfying in answering the question of "how." But I think that I at least know the "why" of the "how." That is, I believe I understand why we cannot answer the question adequately. Like the other poor prisoners, we are still trapped in Plato's cave. What took place on the hill called Golgotha two thousand years ago, as witnessed by those present and those of us who have read about it, was not the reality itself but the mere shadow of the reality. I am not at all trying to trivialize Jesus' horrific death. In fact, I refer the reader to an excellent article in the *Journal of the American Medical Association* titled "On the Physical Death of Jesus Christ" (Edwards, et al., March 21, 1986, vol. 255, no. 11).

As I stated earlier, we have no way of conceiving what happens when a divine and immortal being is subjected to the ultimate form of death—the separation from the divine and immortal source of life.

Once more, let us consider the nature of God and Jesus. In John 1:1–2 we read, "In the beginning was the Word, and the Word was with God, and the Word was God. He was with God in the beginning." John 1:14 describes the relationship between Jesus and man: "The Word became flesh and made his dwelling among us."

The first verse speaks of Jesus being intrinsic to that "God space" I mentioned in Chapter 3 (that is, it is outside the scope of spacetime, always existent, always intrinsic to the "I Am"). In the latter verse, while not losing His first identity, He is also fully human and "in time." Thus, He is the consummate interface between the eternal, all-existent, the illuminated and almighty God, and the transient, flawed, blind, and dark being called man.

I think it is in this context that we need to contemplate Romans 6:6: "For we know that our old self [each of us] was crucified with him" and Ephesians 2:6: "And God raised us up with Christ and seated us with him in the heavenly realms in Christ Jesus."

Note the past tense of the verbs used! It is a real and already accomplished thing, even before you and I came to know existence. This attests to the dumbfounding nature and power of that dual identity as both God and man and how one sacrifice might atone for all transgressions past, present, and future to Jesus' time on earth two thousand years ago.

Further, I think theologians must give an accounting to this reality when considering Ephesians 1:4–5, which says, "For he chose us in him before the creation of the world to be holy and blameless in his sight. In love he predestined us for adoption to sonship through Jesus Christ, in accordance with his pleasure and will," and Deuteronomy 30:19–20, which says, "Now choose life, so that you and your children may live and that you may love the LORD your God"; that is, the intercourse between predestination and free will.

I do not pretend to have the answer; I only point out the truths that should be factored in when analyzing such matters. It is the fact that Jesus, by way of His interface with the eternal, was able to pay the consequence of sins committed by those who did not yet exist, which should give us our greatest confidence in our personal salvation through Him.

No matter how often we may feel as if we have failed in our Christian walk, we know that nothing we do comes as a surprise to God. It states in Proverbs 24:16, "for though the righteous fall seven times, they rise again." This deserves a little commentary. First, realize that "righteous" refers to how God sees us in Christ, not our own merit.

Second, "seven times" does not refer to a literal seven instances. Otherwise, I would have said, "Oh crap, I know that was number eight!" a long time ago. Seven is sometimes referred to as God's number of perfection or completeness. It means "as many as it takes." That is why Jesus used it in Matthew 18:21– 22 to give perspective on the riches of God's grace compared to the legalism of man: "Then Peter came to Jesus and asked, 'Lord, how many times shall I forgive my brother or sister who sins against me? Up to seven times?' Jesus answered, 'I tell you, not seven times, but seventy-seven times.'"

Considering the magnitude of that stage, it would be much more amazing if we were able to have some comprehension of what happened on that hill than it is that we do not. The bottom line is that Jesus had to pay the price for us in temporal time and somehow access that interface with the eternal before He could send—and we could be indwelt by, and our souls survive—the Holy Spirit.

I do not think that we shall remain forever ignorant. Once we have breached that heavenly shore, as one of my favorite literary characters, Agatha Christie's[10] Hercules Poirot, would say, "All will be revealed."

In *Mere Christianity*, C. S. Lewis[11] wrote, "Any theories we build up as to how Christ's death did all this are, in my view, quite secondary: mere plans or diagrams to be left alone if they do not help us, and, if they do not help us, not to be confused with the thing itself." And, as my beautiful and insightful wife stated, "Thankfully, you don't have to know how a computer works in order to use it."

This side of the grave, God continues to give us things to learn and ways to grow. He is preparing us to accept that gift of being finally and forever free of the shackles of humanity and brought to the feast of our perfected natures. We will then be able to bear the presence of His glory and totally filled with the essence that I referred to as the Spirit. As a fine piece of optical glass can transmit the light it encounters to what lies beyond it, so we are to transmit this Radiance of God and fill heaven.

I think it is only then, in that state, that we can hope to gain any real insight into the most profound question of why God would love us to such an incomprehensible degree. These current earthly vessels we inhabit are at best capable of murmuring a humble "thank you" and attempting to stumble along after Him. One of our chief lessons is to learn to rely on His promise to walk with us and sustain us every step of the way. As the psalmist said, "Your word is a lamp for my feet, and a light on my path." (Psalm 119:105)

What implication does God's light have on our new nature in His kingdom? In 1 Corinthians13:10, 12 we read, "But when completeness [perfection] comes, what is in part [imperfect] disappears...Now we see only a reflection as in a mirror; then we shall see face to face." As I alluded to earlier, in order to be made perfect, a part of me must die. You may be wondering, *If part of me is dead, will I still be "me"?*

As opposed to the monistic perspective discussed in chapter two, where we lose our individual identity and become an indistinguishable part of the whole, I think it is of value to again consider the analogy of light bulbs.

Imagine a string of Christmas lights. Now on this string are lights of various sizes and shapes and colors. Take that strand and take it into a dark room and what do you see? Nothing, remember, the room is dark. But what happens if you plug in that string of lights? Well, if the current is low, you may start to see some faint glows. I consider this to be our current state. We have a little light, but the darkness still surrounds us. Now imagine that the current is turned up to full. Suddenly there are red, green, blue, and many other colors. There are large and small and round and oblong shapes. Each one has a unique place on the string and without any one of them the coalesced light would not be complete. So is the kingdom of heaven.

It states in 1 John 1:5 that "God is light; in him there is no darkness at all." Once we are fully illuminated, there is no place for any shadow to take refuge. There is only one redeeming fact about the darkness. When even a little light begins to shine in the blackness, it is readily seen and draws our attention to it.

Earlier I discussed those weapons of darkness that have been used to keep us slaves. What I did not tell you before was what can happen when they are exposed to the amazing power of the light. Temper is transformed to patience, envy to vicarious gladness, lust to love, anxiety to assurance, depression to joy, guilt to forgiveness, doubt to hope, fear to courage, loneliness to community, grief to rejoicing, and condemnation to compassion. Not only will you still be you, but you will be the fully realized you, the you that you were designed and destined to be. Your personality and potential will be maximized. For the first time, and forevermore, you will finally know what it means to be you.

I have discussed *Who* has arranged for this most marvelous fate to befall us and some of His attributes. But what is the nature of the connection that will allow the Spirit to be transmitted? And how will that impact our escaping boredom?

CHAPTER 9

RELATIONSHIP AND THE SEARCH FOR SIGNIFICANCE

"Do you not know that your bodies are temples of the Holy Spirit, who is in you, whom you have received from God?"
1 CORINTHIANS 6:19

"Husbands, love your wives, just as Christ loved the church and gave himself up for her to make her holy, cleansing her by the washing with water through the word, and to present her to himself as a radiant church, without stain or wrinkle or any other blemish, but holy and blameless."
EPHESIANS 5:25–27

Health is the greatest gift, contentment the greatest wealth, faithfulness the best relationship.
BUDDHA

Spiritual relationship is far more precious than physical. Physical relationship divorced from spiritual is body without soul.
MAHATMA GANDHI

To pass from estrangement from God to be a son of God is the basic fact of conversion. That altered relationship with God gives you an

altered relationship with yourself, with your brother man, with nature, with the universe.
E. STANLEY JONES

The skeptic and his wife and another couple were strolling along the avenue after dinner on a pleasant summer evening, discussing all manner of things. One person voiced the question, "Why does the Bible say that there is no marriage in heaven?" The skeptic, not taking full consideration of the circumstance, was quick to offer the ill-advised reply, "Well, after all, it is heaven." The skeptic received a sharp elbow to the ribs from his spouse, and let me tell you, it hurt! I think I got a bruise from that one.

Nevertheless, the question is valid and has tremendous implication with respect to the prospect of becoming bored with heaven.

Over the years, I have become increasingly aware of how wonderful a family I was privileged to be born into. This is not to say that things were always perfect. There were those things plaguing all humans found at our house. There were short tempers, harsh words, hurt feelings, guilt, tears, and times of feeling isolated. But I always had some core belief that through it all, somehow, I had a home where I belonged. Somehow, I had a family where I was loved, if not always in the moment, at least in the final accounting.

I am the youngest of five siblings. My mother was orphaned at the age of ten or so and, as best as I can put it together, she was passed around from one relative to another to be cared for more out of obligation than of love.

Consequently, I don't think she ever really had a feeling of family until she met and married the man with whom she would spend more than five decades—my dad. He was the fourth of ten children that issued from Asa and Mamie Thomas in a small town in western Iowa. I am not sure that he had the best relationship with his dad, but I know he had a decent relationship with his siblings and felt secure in his mom's love. I think she was principally the one from whom he formed the concept of what it is to be family, a concept that he held very dear and demonstrated faithfully, if not always perfectly.

My oldest sibling is my sister, who is twelve years my senior. To her I may owe some of the impetus for writing this book. It was she who, while holding me at age three or four by my heels over the toilet and threatening to flush me down if I didn't quit crying, convinced me to consider the concept of the finality of this life in the first place!

Had I been older I might have realized she wouldn't really carry out this heinous act. I might have reasoned that the chances of her plugging up the toilet would have been extremely high and then she would have been in sooo much trouble. I am happy to state that our relationship has progressed nicely since then and, though she may still at times consider me to be a "turd," I doubt she would ever want to flush me.

My oldest brother is ten years my senior. It is safe to say that he was the sibling I admired most when I was a young boy. He was big and strong, good looking, intelligent, and had one of the best singing voices I had (or have) ever heard. For the most part, I think that he tolerated me. Sure, there was the time he and my next older brother decided to teach me to ride a bicycle by taking me up to the top of the hill on the street in front of our house.

They placed me on his three-speed, twenty-six-inch bicycle with the simple instruction of, "If you want to turn, then turn the wheel that direction and lean a little."

Since my feet were not within six inches of the pedals, I did not have to worry about how to use those. And I guess when it came to "stopping," they thought that I was capable of figuring that out for myself. In a manner of speaking, I did figure it out. All I needed was an impending intersection with cars racing back and forth, a narrow alley just short of that, and a fence bordering the alley just high enough to stop the bike, send me over the fence and onto my back in the neighbor's yard. That I was not seriously injured is testimony to the concept of guardian angels. Even so, that pretty much killed my enthusiasm for bicycle riding for some time.

My next sibling probably had more to do with the solidification of my concept of family than any of the others. Her name was Gretchen Marie Thomas, and she was born in 1945 with what was then termed "mongolism," or, as it is better known today, Down syndrome. At that time, it was common for children born with this disorder to be given over to some long-term care facility. I do not think any the less of parents who opted to do this.

The task of raising a child with special needs was daunting in those days, when there were no resources for long-term independent living when the child became adult. To keep a child like this in the home was tantamount to accepting a lifelong commitment to care. Yet my parents made that commitment without hesitation.

I am virtually positive that my mother (wrongly) felt as if she had done something terrible and that this was God's way of retribution. While I think she sincerely believed in His provision for her to come into His kingdom, I do not believe that she had experienced as a child the baseline of security of what it is to be loved unconditionally in order to take this into the depth of her heart. Mom passed away in 1992 and now knows that truth to a degree that we are unable to fathom.

I can cite many examples of how my parents were committed to Gretchen. My mother essentially gave up her career as a registered nurse to adequately care for Gretchen and the rest of us. But while my other siblings and I would eventually be self-sufficient, Gretchen would not. I believe, had it been otherwise, mom would have resumed her nursing career, a job from which she derived much fulfillment and enjoyment.

Pop showed the brightest as mom's health began to fail. He finally gave up the career he loved to become full-time caregiver to both mom and Gretchen. After mom passed away, he continued dutifully and lovingly to care for Gretchen.

This task became even more difficult as Gretchen developed rapidly progressive Alzheimer's dementia and became essentially a functional invalid. As pop himself, at age 89, once put it, "You know when you only outweigh someone by 30 pounds and they refuse to put their feet on the floor, it is hard to hold them over the toilet and pull their pants down at the same time. My toes just aren't that talented!" I will sum it up by saying that from the moment she was born until the moment she died, Gretchen never knew what it was to be unloved. Her life as part of our family was a significant component of the cement that bonded us in love.

Then there is my next older brother. He was the one with whom I always felt some degree of competition. Being three and one-half years older than I would have been unfair advantage enough, but he had other attributes for which I had no answer. He was the most athletic of the children (in PE class they timed my 100-yard dash with a sundial); he was popular and had (and has) lots of artistic ability. He seemed not to stumble over the things in life that bothered me, like guilt, and did not tolerate such things in me. This made for more than a little conflict.

He once dubbed me "Sister Greg," a moniker that I was happy did not stick. Overall, he seemed to enjoy life more than I could. I remember a birthday card he gave me a few years back. On the cover it said something like, "Do you remember when we were kids and I used to tease you and tie you up and generally make your life miserable?" Then on opening the card it read, "I really miss those days."

Most of the time we got along reasonably well, but I don't remember feeling very loved by him until I was a freshman in college. I was not having a great time of it and was feeling more than a little overwhelmed at the prospect of trying to get through school and into medical school. Additionally, it was my first extended time away from home, and I was homesick. He was in dental school at the time in Portland and made a special trip one weekend for no other reason than to see me. That was special. My brother truly cared enough to do that for me. Our relationship has continued to improve since then, and I have a full sense of acceptance, support, and love with all my siblings. Pop and Mom would have been gratified to know this.

For my part and reflecting on the original question of this chapter, God has seen fit to gift to me a wonderful (if sharp-elbowed) wife named Heidi. It was she who first motivated me to reconsider not only who God is but even if there was a personal God in the first place.

As I wrote earlier, I have not always had a belief in any type of God beyond one that would probably fit in with pantheism, sort of like "the force" in the *Star Wars* movies.[1] My concept of God was quite distorted. How askew? It promoted enough guilt to cause me to spend my early adolescence wondering daily if the earth would open and swallow me. Consequently, finding so little grace, I was anxious, neurotic, and depressed. By my later teen years, I had concluded that if that representation of God was correct, I wanted nothing to do with Him.

As an adult, I have known many people who grew up in the Catholic Church and a have strong, vibrant faith and relationship with God. Alas, somehow, I had missed the boat. It was not until years later, when I met this young lady who had a strength in her that I found most appealing—and it didn't hurt that she was (and is) cute—that I was at all tempted to readdress my concept of the Christian God.

This was not something that I would undertake without great reservation. To investigate along this line would be to potentially bring back the ghosts of unrelenting guilt, shame and fear that had tortured me for those years and land me back in that pit of despair and seemingly inescapable condemnation. On the other hand, she assured me that my previous concepts were markedly incorrect, and, despite my fear, I reasoned that if I was wrong and there is a God out there who really does care about me, then I would be a fool not to look for Him.

We have been granted the privilege of having five wonderful children. (I am happy to report that they are all a definite improvement on the male half of their progenitor prototype.) My wife and I have strived to give them a home and a sense of family that would allow them to face whatever the future may bring their way, knowing that, so long as any of the rest of us were around, they were loved and would not lack a place of security and rest.

My family of origin was always physically demonstrative of affection, and I think this has been successfully transmitted on to the children. Perhaps it is the Italian portion of my ancestry that has made that an integral part of loving others. I made it a goal that by the time they were but a few years old, they would have each been kissed so much that if they were never kissed again and lived to 100, they still would have been kissed more than one time for every day of their lives.

When they were old enough to comprehend this, I shared it with them as a way of reassuring them that they would always be loved. I will not go into how "wonderful, talented, handsome, beautiful, musical, and brilliant" any of my children are. Such things are found in Christmas letters, those rambling seasonal notes you look at and think, "Oh brother, here we go again." I assure you that if you ever receive (or have received) a Christmas letter from us, it will contain nothing of that kind. Suffice it to say, as I tell our children, they are each a blessing beyond measure.

My family has made it easier for me to arrive at a concept of a loving God. Perhaps, because of them, it was easier for me than for many who may be reading this. During my late teen years, I remember telling an acquaintance that I was routinely hugged and kissed by both my parents. He was genuinely astonished. He told me that he could not recall having ever been hugged or kissed by his father. I was equally astonished.

You see, it was not until that point that I began to realize I had been given something through my family that so many people lack: significance in being. I do not know how else one might attain this cornerstone of the psyche other than by being loved. If you were neglected, or physically, sexually, or emotionally abused in your home, my heart goes out to you.

Some who read this may have suffered things happening at the hands of people who were, or at least called themselves, Christians. I don't know what to do for you other than leave this writing and pray that God will let it be a signpost for you—a message to let you know that no matter what the world says, you have worth. You are of such great value that the God of all creation wants to take you into His arms and hold you and dry every tear and replace your emptiness with the fullness of love. I know that this may be a difficult concept to accept, but I will use another analogy to make my point.

I live in Salem, Oregon. If you drive 100 miles due west of my home, you will get very, very wet. Your car and you will both need bodacious snorkels. You don't have to believe this, but that does not alter the fact that what I say is true. Wet is wet. And I assure you that God does love *you*, and that is what ultimately allows you to attain significance.

Beyond the immediate necessities of food, shelter, and whatever is necessary for the continuance of life, I think that our most basic drive is the search for significance. It is the underlying motivator for everything from love to dictatorial power, spirituality to sadism. It is what motivates the body builder to spend hour after hour lifting the same weights up and down. It makes the die-hard sports fan live the entire year anticipating a few brief hours watching "his" team.

In the worst-case scenario, it can empower us to commit acts of violence, perhaps even murder a fan of another team. Some people look for significance in money, social standing, work, being a father or mother, sex, athletic ability, fame, and infamy. It is not that all of these are intrinsically bad. A well-rendered physique, if not overdone, can be a thing of beauty.

Think Michelangelo's[2] sculpture *David*. Money can be used for good things, and power in the proper hands is a blessing. As for sex, well, I didn't get five kids by sitting around trying to stack BBs on a windy day. The downside is that most endeavors result in very transient realized gain. The entire Old Testament book of Ecclesiastes is devoted to pondering this subject. But I think the general concept is captured beautifully in the middle three stanzas of A. E. Housman's[3] poem, "To an Athlete Dying Young":

The time you won your town the race
We chaired you through the market-place;
Man and boy stood cheering by,
And home we brought you shoulder-high.

To-day, the road all runners come,
Shoulder-high we bring you home,
And set you at your threshold down,
Townsman of a stiller town.

Smart lad, to slip betimes away
From fields where glory does not stay
And early though the laurel grows
It withers quicker than the rose.

Eyes the shady night has shut
Cannot see the record cut,
And silence sounds no worse than cheers
After earth has stopped the ears:

Now you will not swell the rout
Of lads that wore their honours out,
Runners whom renown outran
And the name died before the man.

So set, before its echoes fade,
The fleet foot on the sill of shade,
And hold to the low lintel up
The still-defended challenge-cup.

And round that early-laurelled head
Will flock to gaze the strengthless dead,
And find unwithered on its curls
The garland briefer than a girl's.

For any who would place their emphasis elsewhere, few of our pursuits are likely to survive beyond the grave except honest-to-goodness devotional love. Perhaps, if you have heard a few sermons on the subject, you know it better under the term agape. This is a Greek word that carries a dictionary definition of "unselfish, loyal and benevolent concern for the good of another."

This is the type of love of which Jesus was speaking in Matthew 22:37,39 when He said, "Love the Lord your God with all your heart and with all your soul and with all your mind.... Love your neighbor as yourself." As opposed to the noun love, which can mean any number of things, I am writing about the verb form that is best transmitted through relationship. And that relationship must be genuine if it is going to let others know that they are significant to us.

Regrettably, I am very much an introvert. While some people are comfortable in a crowd, in such a gathering I am about as much at ease as a balloon at a convention of porcupines. Consequently, real relationship would virtually never arise out of a confluence of people with whom I was not already acquainted.

While I crave at least brief times of solitude, there are few people that I will get bored with faster than me. When I have my siblings, spouse, children, or friends around, most of the time, things are going to be somehow a little more exciting, a little more enjoyable.

Now, in Christian circles, there is this thing called *fellowship*, and my next older brother and I absolutely dread it. For example, many years ago, my wife belonged to a women's Bible study group. The ladies of the group decided that it would be "fun" to have an evening of "fellowship," at which everyone would bring their spouses. Despite my reluctance to venture forth into such circumstance, I acquiesced to my spouse's wishes and went.

As I anticipated, when we got there, I knew my wife and one other couple. The thirty other people there were complete strangers. I am not much for making small talk when there is no subject of note. I learned a long time ago not to ask someone, "How are you?" Being a physician, I can tell you that, once people know what I do for a living, they will tell me exactly how they are.

Since I don't have a medical practice in the local Safeway store, I don't really want to hear about someone's latest hemorrhoidal flair while I search for frozen peas. Probably the photographic exhibit at the state fair is not the best place to hear about one's spouse's vaginal discharge.

In any case, I soon ran out of people to "talk" to. While people were being rounded up to play some games and I was silently praying, *Lord, spare me!* I spied a darkened stairway. Since I was not busy "fellowshipping," I made my getaway. At the bottom of the stairs, I found a most delightful room —a library. There was a pleasant glow from a solitary lamp next to an overstuffed chair. It did not take me long to turn my suffering into the much more enjoyable experience of reading. I do not remember what I read. I only know that the material was of some interest, and I was not feeling the strain of forced social interaction.

My reverie lasted for over an hour, and though I knew there would be a price extracted by my wife for my behavior, or as Red Skelton's4 "mean little kid" used to say, "If I dood it, I get a whippin'. I dood it!" I made my choice.

When I was finally found out (apparently, they did a mass search for the corpus delicti), I got exactly what I expected, an in-private but prolonged tongue lashing. But just when things were darkest, God arranged a great ray of hope to flash into my life. It came with my wife's final words: "And I'm never going to take you to a gathering like that again!" As Brer Rabbit supposedly said, "Oh please, Brer Bear, don't, promise me you won't ever throw me in the briar patch!" That night I slept well.

Now you could rightly argue that I did not demonstrate any agape-type love in that instance. I confess my shortcoming in that circumstance. As a fallen human, I find it difficult to manufacture enthusiasm and hypocritical to pretend to do so. I am sure I need to improve my attitude in this regard. I am also sure that there will be no need to create a positive outlook on my interactions with others once I get to heaven. Then I can finally attain God's perspective on His children, transmitting His love and attesting to their significance.

The reason there will not be any marriage in heaven is that every relationship we have there will be so much deeper, so much more intimate, so much more comfortable than anything we have ever experienced here. Our most intimate relationships here don't begin to compare with it. As much as I love my wife, children, brothers and sisters, parents, and friends, I will love them so much more in heaven. The thing is that my love will not be confined to just them; it will be profound for every other of my fellow heavenly cohabitants.

My brother (the one who "loves fellowship" as much as I do) once said that he hoped heaven was exceedingly large because there were some people who were going to be there that he really did not want to run into. Not to worry. Once we are free of those aspects of our current humanity that hinder us in our ability to relate to other people, relationship in the form of true fellowship will flow as naturally as water does down a brook.

So, how does this all fit into the search for significance? Well, as I said, our relationship to others will be such that no one will be, or even feel, insignificant. But that is only the beginning of the story. I have become increasingly convinced that the reason we were designed in the first place was to come into a direct and loving relationship with God. Short of that, I do not think that eternal contentment is possible.

As Psalm 42:1–2 puts it, "As the deer pants for streams of water, so my soul pants for you, my God. My soul thirsts for God, for the living God." It states in the Hebrews 1:3 that Jesus is, "the radiance of God's glory and the exact representation of his being." Then in 1 John, it is stated, "When Christ appears, we shall be like him" (3:2) and "We should be called children of God!" (3:1).

This relationship with God is our ultimate destiny, the principal reason for which we were created, and the final answer to why we will never be bored in eternity. This is the core of significance that can never grow tedious. The New Testament has extensive descriptions about how Christ is the head, and we are the body. Christ is the cornerstone, and we are the rest of the temple of God. It states in 1 Corinthians 3:21–23, "All things are yours... and you are of Christ, and Christ is of God."

Once we are plugged into Christ, our anchoring point, and He, fully illuminated, into the Father, we will know what it is to be whole and content. No more looking around for substitutes. The light bulb will have finally found the socket, been put in place, and turned blazingly on, never to dim again. We will realize our significance beyond measure in our relationship with God.

"And I pray that you, being rooted and established in love, may have power, together with all the Lord's holy people, to grasp how wide and long and high and deep is the love of Christ, and to know this love that surpasses knowledge—that you may be filled to the measure of all the fullness of God" (Ephesians 3:17–19).

What will this Spirit energy flow look like? To gain the briefest glimpse, I think it useful to consider the attributes of God. God is beyond eternal. God is life.

Recall the analogy about the DVD and the one who created it. God exists outside the boundaries of time. He cannot age. The Bible attests to Jesus transmitting the Spirit of God and to us being like Him and in Him. It would be impossible for us to age, to not have eternal life when we are likewise the filled vessels of that Spirit.

He is the author of love. In Galatians 5:22, the very first aspect of the fruit of the Spirit listed is love. To be the conduit of that type of love is beyond my imagination.

Using a mechanism frequently employed by God, perhaps we can gain the faintest glimmer of what it is to be fully embodied by, or integrated with, the Holy Spirit. I would like you to consider a dream I once had.

In the opening scene, a man was standing alone in a large, subtly sunlit auditorium. There was dark, beautiful wood paneling. Everything was quiet and still. The man began to sing. The first note was strong and pure, like a well-struck chime. As he continued, something most unusual happened; his body began to resonate with the sound. To understand what I am saying, consider a Stradivarius violin. Imagine what it would be like to be that instrument in the hands of the master musician, to feel the music reverberating through your entire being. The music is not about the instrument, but instead the instrument is entirely about the music. It felt incredibly exhilarating, and what happened next was just as curious.

The entire hall also began to resonate with the sound. Everything was in perfect accord. It was music that I am sure I will never hear again this side of heaven. I then awoke, moved to the point of tears forming in my eyes.

There are two things I have not yet told you. The music I heard consisted of one persisting note and the lyric of one sustained word. That word was "joy." What the man, what I had experienced, was the essence of joy. I believe I was given a musical foretaste of communing with the Spirit. This is not a matter of talking to, but being indwelt by, the nature of God.

If this example makes any sense to you, then again consider what it would be like to be integrated with God through Christ and thus the Spirit. We will simultaneously transmit and receive, through each other and back to God, His attributes such as love, holiness, peace, and, of course, joy. To have that intimacy will be the ultimate fellowship. I am so looking forward to experiencing God's laugh.

As I have referred, He is the source of true light. What will it be to know that wherever we look, whether without or (even more importantly to my prospects of being able to find sanctuary in eternity) within ourselves, we shall have no fear of finding shadow? Then we will find perfect peace, perfect rest, and contentment—home at last. Perhaps, if I am granted time to do so while still in this shell, I will write again specifically to explore the attributes of God and how they might relate to us given this schema. For now, I shall let it suffice that, as I endeavored to describe earlier in the book, He is beyond all dimensions. He is literally and utterly fathomless—there is no ending to His depth.

So, how did I, and how might you, go about procuring this kind of eternity? To do so must be incredibly complex and difficult, right?

When it comes to accessing God, some people try to make it sound much more complicated than it is. All that is required is a realization that God loves you to an incredible extent, that He wants—and, in fact, pleads— to have you come into His arms, and that He and His Son and the Spirit have provided the only possible route of letting Him make you His beloved child. Having done this, simply and with thanksgiving, talk to God and acknowledge your failure to fulfill His moral law (i.e., your sin nature and consequent acts of sin).

Ask for His incomparable gift of salvation, acknowledging that Jesus has paid your consequence. Accept it, earnestly asking Him to guide your path both now and forever.

That's it. Welcome to the family. Eternity in heaven simply for the asking. If it were not true, it would be too good to be true. In Matthew 7:8 Jesus said, "For everyone who asks receives; he who seeks finds; and to him who knocks, the door will be opened."

In Matthew 11:28–30 the invitation is, "Come to me, all you who are weary and burdened, and I will give you rest. Take my yoke upon you and learn from me, for I am gentle and humble in heart, and you will find rest for your souls. For my yoke is easy and my burden is light."

John 6:37 says, "Whoever comes to me I will never drive away."

Finally, John 10:28–30 tells us: "I give them eternal life, and they shall never perish; no one will snatch them out of my hand. My Father, who has given them to me, is greater than all; no one can snatch them out of my Father's hand. I and the Father are one."

It is not me giving you these assurances; it is the One who loves you enough to have paid the price for you.

There is another step that I strongly encourage you to take if you have decided to take advantage of this amazing gift. As you have read above, the reality of eternity is based in relationship with God and then with others.

Shortly after talking with God, tell someone who is a Christian about your decision. If they give you a blank stare, then consider the possibility that this person may not actually know what you are talking about and indeed may not be a Christian. Proceed directly to tell someone else.

On the other hand, if their face lights up, and they get a big smile and say something like, "Yes! I've been praying for you for years!" and immediately want to pray with you, giving thanks for you, they most likely are a Christian.

Please do not take offense if something of that nature is said to you. It does not imply that until that point the person saw you as a "worthless heathen," somehow unfit to be in their "holy presence." Quite the contrary, a Christian who truly realizes their faith has already had the experience of being where you are. He or she previously recognized that they have a multitude of flaws, imperfections, and shortcomings. That person has already gained appreciation of having no basis to stand before a holy God without that single intervention of God incarnated as a man to make it possible.

Look for that person to be genuinely thrilled by your passing from sure death to eternal life. Don't be surprised if there are a few tears of joy. From my personal experience, I can tell you that it is as if my somewhat calloused "heart" was suddenly submerged in a vat of meat tenderizer.

The person who responds to you in this way can probably put you in touch with a group of believers who can help you learn more about this incredible journey. It will not take long to discover that, though God now sees you as perfect through Christ, you are a diamond in the rough. That family of believers will guide, encourage, and support you, bracing you as you start to grow straight and tall.

It is also of extreme importance that you let God Himself give you guidance, and the best way to do that is to start regularly reading His Word, the Bible. For my part, I remember being served very well by starting in the book of John, where I think you will find that many of the concepts I discussed in this book surface quickly.

A cautionary note: Like you, even much more established believers are not yet perfect. There is only one perfect Christian in this life, and His name is Jesus. If anyone tells you something different, consider that person an unreliable source. I am very much a work in progress, as you could easily learn by speaking with my wife, children, siblings, in-laws, friends, coworkers, patients, our marriage counselor ("Larry, fix me!"), pastors, or even the guy who flipped me the bird today as I traveled down the highway. (I did refrain from responding in kind—this time.)

That brings me to a few words on a topic of paramount importance to God—forgiveness and mercy. We have just contemplated the incredible chasm between God's Holiness and our lack of it. Once we comprehend how much love and forgiveness God has shown, it should motivate us to extend love and forgiveness to others. Do you need to forgive anyone even a tiny fraction of what God has forgiven you?

In Matthew 2:7, Jesus shows the importance of forgiveness by quoting from Hosea 6:6, which states, "I desire mercy, not sacrifice." I will illustrate this point by way of a parable Jesus tells in Matthew 25:14–30. If you have a Bible available, then please take a moment to familiarize yourself with the text.

Those whom God places in our lives are like bags of unrefined silver. The more closely He has placed the raw treasure to us, the greater the responsibility we have for it. Thus, our parents, siblings, spouses, and children are at one level of accountability, our friends and acquaintances at another, and then less for more distant peoples. Yet no matter how far removed, we still have some accountability for the rest of humanity.

God has seen fit to give us an incredible power, one sought by wizards and wise men for eons. It is called alchemy. It is the ability to change one element into another. We exercise this power with special tools that God has given us: the unquenchable fire of love, the melting bowl of forgiveness, and the alloy of mercy. If we take the raw silver and pour it into the bowl of forgiveness, heat it with the fire of love, and then add the essential alloy of mercy, we will assist the Master Metallurgist in transmuting the adulterated silver into the purest of gold. We will take part in creating spirits that are alive, vibrant, and full of peace, harmony, and love for God and other people.

But proceed with caution. If we fail to use those measures by withholding them, or even worse, use other tools like the fire of anger, the bowl of revenge, and the alloy of self- righteousness, we will turn that silver into lead. We will be held responsible for producing spirits that are pain-ridden, self-absorbed, hateful, and cold toward God and man.

Eventually, all of us will have to return to God the treasure that He entrusted to our care. At that time, those who committed themselves to Christ as their Savior and Lord will be separated from those who are Christian in name only, those unwilling to truly follow His example. The book of James has much to say about mercy and true Christian behavior. James 2:17 implies that faith by itself, if not accompanied by action, is "lead".

As He hung on the cross dying for our transgressions, Jesus set the ultimate example for us when He said, "Father, forgive them, for they do not know what they are doing" (Luke 23:34). What will be in the bags you return to the Master? If you have accepted

His offer and provision of forgiveness, then give thanks to God and obey His will: freely forgive.

Realize there will be times when, though you are Christian, you will fall. Further realize that you are still a child of God, and if you honestly desire forgiveness and help, God will be there to pick you up again. It has been my experience that the more often I fall, the easier it is for me to call even my salvation into doubt. It is then I most need a spiritual and scriptural anchor. I look to three sets of verses. These two verses in Romans remind me that my salvation does not rely on my efforts to be holy, but wholly depends on the finished work of God through Christ's propitiation on my behalf:

Therefore, there is now no condemnation for those who are in Christ Jesus, because through Christ Jesus the law of the Spirit who gives life has set you free from the law of sin and death.
ROMANS 8:1–2

Who will bring any charge against those whom God has chosen? It is God who justifies.
ROMANS 8:33

Those verses may satisfy the intellect, but the heart can still be fettered to the burden. That is why Hebrews 10:22 is essential to my gaining peace in those situations: "Let us draw near to God with a sincere heart and with the full assurance that faith brings, having our hearts sprinkled to cleanse us from a guilty conscience." Note that having our hearts sprinkled does not refer to cleansing us from the sin per se; that was already accomplished as above. Instead, it acts to cleanse the guilty conscience, that accusatory voice that would still bind the emotion in slavery to guilt. I encourage you to memorize this verse and use it in those trials to find rest for your soul.

You will probably find that you want to tell others about your decision. It is difficult not to talk about what excites us. My sister-in-law, Susie, illustrated that point as a child when, as December 25 was approaching, she blurted out to her father, "Daddy, you'll never guess what color brown pants you're getting for Christmas!"

I was once told that a good essay should be like a good miniskirt: long enough to cover the essentials but short enough to keep it interesting. Hopefully, I have not violated that precept with this book. My desire is that the book has helped you gain a new understanding and appreciation of the Christian faith in general and the importance of cultivating an eternal perspective on our existence—one that will assist as you face the trials, temptations, and tedium of this life.

The Apostle Paul was imprisoned multiple times, sentenced five times to thirty-nine lashes, beaten with rods three times, stoned once and left for dead, and shipwrecked three times. He knew danger, hunger, thirst, nakedness, and cold. According to church tradition, he was eventually martyred for his faith. However, he must have mastered this eternal perspective. In 2 Corinthians 4:17–18 he wrote, "For our light and momentary troubles are achieving for us an eternal glory that far outweighs them all. So, we fix our eyes not on what is seen, but on what is unseen, since what is seen is temporary, but what is unseen is eternal." Light and momentary troubles indeed. I pray that you and I might be able to grasp and utilize this same truth.

In closing, Jesus once said that the greatest of the commandments are to love God with all your heart, strength, mind, and spirit, and your neighbor as yourself. Once we are irrevocably attached to the Creator in this manner and His Spirit is surging through our being, the natural, the inescapable result is that it flows through us and out to others. It seems to me that Jesus was not only speaking about a "good way" to lead our lives here but was actually alluding to the eternal reality that awaits all who come into his kingdom.

It was once stated to me by one of my mentors that it was possible that we existed only as thoughts in the mind of God. I confess that this seemed more than a little abstract to me at the time. However, as I have now had sufficient time to digest that more thoroughly, I have come to appreciate just how un-abstract that statement may be. I don't think that it makes much difference if we consider a secular spontaneous event or a monotheistic creation scenario. The fact remains that the energy came into being i.e. was created (causation). Also, I consider it at least as logical to contemplate that something could disappear into nothing as it is to entertain the idea that something could spring into existence from nothing. (So much for the first law of thermodynamics that governs this universe.) So, if creation of that primal energy is possible, on that same scale I would reason that "un-creation" is plausible. Relativity tells us that neither time or physical dimensionality is absolute. Quantum mechanics states that there is a minimal size, Planck length, below which nothing can exist in this universe, except as a probability. Thus, I find my thoughts on what is "real" reduced to the only thing left, the one thing that exists outside of and independent of spacetime/ creation – God. We are told in John 4:24, Psalm 51:11 and other places that God is spirit. God is the ultimate reality. Therefore, the spiritual realm makes our universe illusory by comparison. He thought (willed) our cosmos into being. As He is outside of spacetime, and therefore not subject to it, so are His thoughts. Indeed, His thoughts define what our reality is.

I look forward to that place called heaven, where I can finally be me and you will be who you were intended to be. We absolutely will not experience boredom. We will know what it is to be finally home, basking in the Light. Then we will realize perfect peace, filled with unbounded and unending joy, significant in the best way possible by virtue of our relationship with our Creator and each other. May God bless you on your journey. My prayer for you is several millennia old and found in Numbers 6:24–26: "The LORD bless you and keep you; the LORD make his face shine on you and be gracious to you; the LORD turn his face toward you and give you peace."

EPILOGUE

I thank all of those who have encouraged me in the writing of this small book. My heartfelt appreciation to all who have supported me, prayed for me, befriended me, put up with me, and often, forgiven me as I have stumbled along this journey.

I thank my parents, my siblings, my children, and in-laws, my childhood and adult friends and, in particular, my wife. Each has given me some grasp of what it is to be significant to them and loved unconditionally.

My thanks to my primary editor, Sue Miholer, who transformed many of my paragraph pages into pages of paragraphs. I also extend my appreciation to my publisher, who graciously considered publishing an unknown writer and aided me in creating comprehensible sentences and cutting waste. Also, my thanks to my patients who have entrusted me with the care and the well-being of their loved ones over the past several decades. Much of what I have written was meant to supplement the things that I wished we had time to talk about during those frenetic office rendezvous.

I thank my seventh-grade English teacher, Mrs. Fischer, who, after reading one of my essays and chuckling, took me aside and told me that I should consider doing something with writing when I "grew up." I was a little slow, but at the age of seventy, I guess I'm nearly full grown.

Most of all, my thanks go to my Lord and Savior, who loved me enough to pay my ransom at His great expense and in His mercy has granted me some small glimpse of His glory and, hopefully, some tiny part in letting others know of His great love for them.

APPENDIX A

TIME, DIMENSIONS, AND GOD; A MATHEMATICIAN'S PERSPECTIVE

I realize that for some readers, my treatise may seem vastly oversimplified and not worthy of any intellectual consideration. For those of you who require more academic horsepower to stimulate your nimble brains (after all, one donkey is not even one horsepower!) I have arranged, with his permission, to include a snippet of more erudite writing from another author, who goes by the *nom de plume* of A. B. Christian. He is the most intelligent man and one-half of the most intelligent and well-read couple I have ever encountered.

At about the time I felt compelled to write this book, he was, unbeknownst to me, feeling a similar compulsion to address challenges that the "young-adult Christian reader" might encounter—especially those heading onto schooling beyond the compulsory first twelve years. He entitled his work *A Pilgrim's Defense*. In it he addresses challenges to the Christian faith ranging from science and its impact on our faith, to arguments for and against the existence of God, to the historicity of the Bible and of Jesus in particular. He includes thorough appendices and an extensive bibliography. That there are individuals of the scholarly caliber of these persons who find as much validity in the Christian faith as I do, serves as a great encouragement to me.

After reading my chapter on time, my sometimes mentor offered the following insights. In deference to me, he has simplified his thoughts on the subject and left out all but the most basic mathematical constructs. If you find the following more to your level of scholastic appetite, I strongly encourage you to seek out his book, which is available on **Amazon.com.**

As Augustine said, time is a difficult concept. He went on to note that the concept of time seems to require the concept of motion— without motion, there is no time. Fifteen centuries later, Hermann Minkowski was the first to think of time and our three space-like dimensions as four equal dimensions governed by the laws of Special Relativity. Minkowski developed the mathematics needed to describe these as a four-dimensional manifold (in three dimensions this could be thought of as a box). If we use Spinoza's idea of there being only two dimensions in our world, extension and duration, now called space and time, we can draw a Minkowski diagram of the world as:

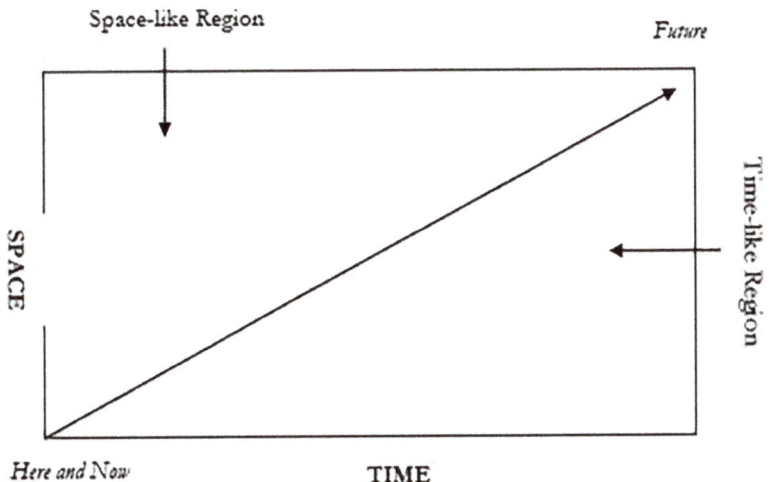

155

In this diagram, the units have been chosen so that the speed of light is one unit. The origin in the diagram represents the "here and now." The arrow proceeding from the origin at a thirty-eight degree angle represents the path of light (a photon). A line (path) starting at the origin and moving to the right is called *time-like* if it remains below the diagonal and *space-like* if it remains above the diagonal. Each person's life is represented by a very small squiggly line moving from left to right, his (her) world line, in the lower triangle of the diagram. It is not possible for the world line or any other realizable path to cross the diagonal since this would imply a velocity greater than the speed of light in a vacuum.

The Minkowski diagram cannot directly be applied to the case of General Relativity. There are several reasons for this, one being that space is probably not what mathematicians call *simply connected*. In simpler terms, there are "holes" in space. Physicists have written about black holes, white holes, and worm holes. In the diagram, it would appear that a time-like path could be traced from any point in the lower triangle to any other, as long as it does not cross the diagonal. But a path in spacetime (Minkowski's term) cannot traverse such holes. However, mathematical physicists have devised analogous, but more complicated diagrams to represent the world as a two-dimensional diagram: one looks a little like a checkerboard with all the squares of one-color missing. The important point is that there is no movement in any of these diagrams. A Minkowski-type diagram is not a moving picture of what is happening moment by moment but is a *static* picture of the entire world (universe) from the origin (big bang, Genesis) to the future (end of the age, Revelation).

Einstein's equations describe what we know for a world (universe) dominated by the force of gravity. This world has four dimensions, three space-like and one time-like. There have been a few successful solutions of these equations, starting with the three solutions of Friedmann in 1924, the year before he died, (at) age 37.

Gödel later discovered a solution in which a realizable path in spacetime had the form of a loop—i.e., in which time travel to the past would be possible. This particular solution did not describe our universe, but the fact that such a solution of Einstein's equations was possible implies either that: 1) time travel is possible; or 2) Einstein's equations are not the final description of reality. Probably most people think that time travel is not possible, since there are so many well-known contradictions, and no known solutions for avoiding those contradictions. This also means, we think, that the physicists' concept of time is not the final word on the concept of time.

Maybe the way forward is to add dimensions. Spinoza, in his *Ethics*, "proved" that God exists in an infinite number of dimensions —why limit Him? String theory needs eleven dimensions, one time-like, the others space-like. Why not add more dimensions to accommodate concepts like mind, soul, spirit, and so on, and also to accommodate concepts such as psychological time (the type illustrated by the bicycle story)? That is, instead of advancing to n space-like dimensions and one time-like dimension, we could advance to n space-like dimensions and m time-like dimensions.

Before continuing, however, let us look at a case involving *fewer* dimensions. In 1884, Edwin A. Abbott, using the *nom de plume* A. Square, wrote a book called *Flatland*. This book described a world with two space-like dimensions and one time-like dimension. The inhabitants of Flatland had the shapes of n-sided polygons. The lowest class consisted of triangular citizens, and the higher the class, the larger the n, so that the nobility approached a circular shape. Regular polygons were considered superior to others. The relevant episode concerns a sphere, initially located above the plane of Flatland. One day, the sphere began slowly to descend until it intersected Flatland. At first, the denizens of Flatland were amazed at the sudden appearance of a perfect baby—i.e., a small, perfect circle. They crowded around to look and admire, but as the sphere descended further, they had to back up and keep backing up in order to stay out of the circle's way. But then, this perfect being, the like of which no one in flatland had ever before been seen, started shrinking as the sphere kept descending, until at last the circle became a point and then disappeared. The inhabitants of Flatland had no idea of what had happened.

Recall from elementary or high school, that for a point (x,y) in a plane, the square of the distance from the origin (0,0) to that point is given by:

$$d^2 = x^2 + y^2$$

Which is just the Pythagorean theorem. This can be generalized to the distance between two points by the differences—i.e., using $(x - x)^2$ instead of x^2, and so on. This can also be generalized to a point in three dimensions (x,y,z), in which case the square of the distance from the origin is:

$$d^2 = x^2 + y^2 + z^2$$

And to four dimensions (w,x,y,z), in which case the square of the distance from the origin is:

$$d^2 = w^2 + x^2 + y^2 + z^2$$

These equations all assume that the geometry is Euclidean and that the dimensions are space-like dimension. What about time as a dimension? We often give distances in terms of time rather than space – e.g., we might say either "we live ten minutes from church" or "we live three miles from church." Does this mean that time can be thought of as just another dimension, on equal footing with the other three? To answer this, we need to go back to Minkowski. Minkowski was a colleague of Einstein and taught Einstein much of the mathematics needed for the two theories of relativity. For Special Relativity, Minkowski derived the following equation for the distance, now called by physicists the *spacetime interval,* from the origin to a point, now called by physicists an event (x, y, z, t):

$$d^2 = x^2 + y^2 + z^2 - (ct)^2$$

Where c is the speed of light in a vacuum, this is often normalized by choosing units such that the $c=1$. This "distance" equation, called the *Minkowski metric*, was derived from the requirement that the spacetime interval between two events must remain the same under a rotation of the axes; this invariance was a requirement of Special Relativity. The Minkowski metric is quite different from the previous equations. In particular, the "distance" between two events separated in both space and time, could, because of the minus sign in the equation, be zero or even a negative number.

We end this digression by observing that this has thus far been just mathematics—whether or not the Minkowski metric can be applied is another question, one for physicists. The case for Special Relativity has been tested, and the Minkowski metric has been confirmed. For General Relativity, of which Special Relativity is a special case, the Minkowski metric is a good approximation when the gravitational field is very weak, but it does not hold if the world line passes near massive objects such as stars or galaxies.

We have not offered a definition of time, nor are we going to, but we can conclude that time is different, very different, from space. This difference is manifested primarily with the minus sign in the equation. Perhaps someone will someday find a way to generalize the Minkowski metric to handle n space-like dimensions and m time-like dimension, with the distinction between the two types simply being indicated by the sign in front of the normalized dimensions.

In our case, we suggest that reality consists of more than the standard number of dimensions, and that some of the new dimensions are time-like. This would address several problems:

• Theophanies. This would explain how, in the Old Testament, God just suddenly appears, as if He had just stepped out from behind a curtain. Instead, somewhat analogous to the sphere in Flatland, a three-dimensional human form assumed by God would just appear in (be projected into) our three space-like dimensions.

• The continuity problem for the soul. When a person dies, his body may well decompose, with the individual molecules being dispersed throughout the world. God is going to furnish all believers with a resurrection body, but what about the soul—how does the new body get the correct old soul? If there is both a new body and a new soul, how can this be the same person? If the old soul animates the new body upon the death of the old, does this obviate resurrection and the judgment? There is no problem if the original person occupied more than four dimensions, with one new space-like dimension containing the soul and continuing to exist after the associated body's death until needed.

• The mind-body problem. The physical brain is the substratum for thought and memory, but no one has been able sufficiently to localize those attributes anywhere in the brain or any other part of the body; in particular, no one has discovered the location of a person's long-term memory. Maybe the memories are in portions of another space-like dimension associated with the standard three-dimensional body.

• The apparent time dilation during some events. Maybe psychological time is located in a time-like dimension separate from that of physicists' time.

• Angels. In the Bible, the angels, including Satan, often seem unable to foresee the future. Maybe they experience our time-like dimension so that God, but not the angels, can see our world as something analogous to a Minkowski diagram. Similarly, the angels cannot read our thoughts; God, but not the angels, has access to the dimension(s) in which our thoughts are stored.

• Heaven. Heaven may occupy one or more dimensions (of both kinds), probably not including our single time- like dimension, but possibly including our three space-like dimensions. Hence, eternity is outside of time as we know it, and may be larger and more different than we can imagine, with our current four dimensions too few to be interesting in the hereafter.

• God. Even though God is outside of time as we know it, He could, as written throughout the Bible, interact with it. Just as the inhabitants of Flatland could not understand the sphere, so we do not and probably cannot, understand the details of how this could be done.

This approach must not be thought of as pantheism, since all these dimensions could exist as "thoughts" in the mind of God.

161

This theory would be something like Bishop Berkeley's version of empiricism. (Nothing exists unless it is being observed—*esse est percepi*—but God is always observing the world, so we don't have to worry about objects arbitrarily appearing and disappearing.) This is consistent with many scientists coming to the conclusion that the fundamental substance of the world is not matter but mind.

This proposed solution does have one very serious problem, however. There is currently no way to show how a new dimension could interact with the old ones without being detected by experimental physicists—i.e., by detecting a transfer of energy from new to old and vice versa. This problem has long been recognized for the case of the mind-body problem. Descartes postulated that the body and soul were two separate entities, two different types of substance, which operated in an unexplained but coordinated manner. This is a strong form of philosophical dualism. It may be that this problem has been solved—Descartes gave the best possible defense— or it may be that the problem cannot be solved for the same reason. [*That is, if you believe Descartes then you accept his thesis as valid. If you do not think him correct, then the solution may be unobtainable.*] It may also be that there is room for energy (information) to pass from old to new and back undetected by physicists because of the ontological uncertainty inherent in quantum mechanics and/or of the extremely short horizon of predictability in certain chaotic processes. Talk about a god of the gaps! For this reason, we believe that some other explanation needs to be found. Several recent papersbcd have thrown doubt on the very existence of Dark Matter; it may have been explained away. Perhaps the sought-for energy can come from the remaining dark unknown, Dark Energy.

One possible solution [*to possible energy sources that could facilitate the transfer of information between dimensions*] is that the required energy can be found as vacuum energy, the energy contained in the vacuum throughout space. Even if all particles and all electromagnetic energy could be removed from a volume of space, that space would not be empty. There would still, according to Dirac and the Heisenberg uncertainty principle, be pairs of particles and anti-particles, and there would also be three kinds of something called a Zero Point Field, which is a non-zero minimum fluctuation of a quantum field. This vacuum energy is also a candidate for Dark Energy, which could then be the cosmological constant of Einstein's equation. (It may also be a candidate for confirmation that there is a parallel universe close by, but that is another story.)

Some physicists disagree that this could be the cosmological constant because the value of the vacuum energy is too small. However, the value of the vacuum energy has not yet been determined to everyone's satisfaction. There are different ways in which it can be defined and calculated, and the results range from about zero to infinite. The smallest finite numeric result differs from the largest by 120 orders of magnitude—e.g., by a factor of 10^{120}. Most physicists seem to prefer a relatively small value, which would eliminate this as a candidate for Dark Energy and, maybe, the cosmologic constant. However, it is still probably a positive value, and no one knows how much energy would be required to move information between dimensions.

Polkinghorne[e] said that mathematicians are more comfortable with these extra dimensions than physicists are. That may be true, but as with all matter of physics, it is up to the physicists to determine precisely what makes sense, what can be tested, and how results could distinguish between the many different theories that have been proposed.

FOOTNOTES

a. Gödel, Kurt. "A Remark about the Relationship between Relativity Theory and Idealistic Philosophy," in Schilpp, Paul Arthur, ed., *The Library of Living Philosophers, v. VII: Albert Einstein, Philosopher-Scientist, LaSalle, Illinois*: Open Court Publishing Company, 1949.

b. "Astronomers' Doubt About the Dark Side: Errors in Big Bang Data Larger Than Thought?" ScienceDaily.com. 13 June 2010.**http://www.sciencedaily.com//releases/2010/06/10061 3212708.htm**

c. "Vast Structure of Satellite Galaxies Discovered: Do the Milky Way's Companions Spell Trouble for Dark Matter?" ScienceDaily.com. 25 April 2012. **http://www/sciencedaily. com/releases/2012/04/120425094352. htm**

d. "Serious Blow to Dark Matter: New Study Finds Mysterious Lack of Dark Matter in Sun's Neighborhood." ScienceDaily.com. 18 April 2012. **http://www.sciencedaily. com/releases/2012/04/120418111923. htm**

e. Polkinghorne, John. *Science and Religion in Quest of Truth.* New Haven, Connecticut: Yale University Press, 2011.

APPENDIX B

WHO IS REALLY TO BLAME FOR THE DEATH OF JESUS?

It seems that for much of the past two thousand years, much of the focus on reasons to hate Jews has focused on the supposed premise that "they murdered Jesus." It gives me pause to ponder what excuse to hate Jews was used prior to the crucifixion event on that hill called Golgotha ("the place of the skull"). Not that people ever need much of an excuse to hate someone else. There was an old song recorded by the Kingston Trio called "Rioting in Africa." The lyric stated that most groups of people hated other groups of people and some people just did not like anybody.

Hence, we find it easy for the white to hate the black (and the converse), the Chinese to hate the Japanese (and the converse), the short to hate the tall, the woman to hate the man and the Beaver to hate the Duck (Oregon State and University of Oregon, for those of you not from my neck of the woods). There is plenty of hate to go around. It is not that there are not sometimes very good reasons for one group to hate another. What slave would not hate the group that enslaved them, beat them, ravished their women, and murdered their young? The Jews under the heel of the Pharaohs for four hundred years (remember, the United

States of America has only existed for 246 years so far) must have harbored exceptionally acrid bitterness toward their "masters."

No, the singling out of Jews as an object of derision did not start a mere two thousand years ago. According to Judaism Online, there are at least six historical explanations offered for this discrimination; and I think that many of them can be traced back at least as far as the time of bondage in Egypt.

1. ECONOMIC— "We hate Jews because they possess too much wealth and power."

2. CHOSEN PEOPLE— "We hate Jews because they arrogantly claim that they are the chosen people."

3. SCAPEGOAT— "Jews are a convenient group to single out and blame for our troubles."

4. DEICIDE— "We hate Jews because they killed Jesus."

5. OUTSIDERS— "We hate Jews because they are different than us" (the dislike of the unlike).

6. RACIAL THEORY— "We hate Jews because they are an inferior race."

Of these stated reasons, I would venture to say that the economic and outsiders have been closest to the black heart of the matter. Not many of us are totally free of jealousy of someone else's success. Edwin Arlington Robinson's poem "Richard Cory" comes to mind.

Couple that kind of perceived success with an exclusivity where non-Jewish people were not allowed to fully participate in that triumph, and you have a recipe for jealousy of ferocious magnitude.

Yet even that is not the true core of the matter. To find that, we must go back very far, indeed to Genesis 3:15: "And I will put enmity between you and the woman, and between your offspring and hers." Satan has had an unquenchable malevolence for mankind in general and especially the Jews, ever since and probably predating that time. The reason for this is the knowledge that through man in general and the offspring of Abraham and Sarah in particular, would come the One who would defeat and dethrone him as Prince of this world.

In Genesis 12:3, where God is speaking to Abram (later renamed Abraham) we read, "And *all* peoples on earth will be blessed through *you*" (emphasis mine). Of course, the devil would not go down without a fight, but by the providence of God, his fate was sealed. Even now, as his time draws short, he will do his best to avoid the inevitable and, if nothing else, take as many down with him as he can.

Hence, it appears that the stated reasons people give are not the cause for the hatred so much as the *excuse* for it. In this case I wonder how many times "Christ killer" was used as justification for all sorts of evil perpetrated against Jews by those who were not actually even believers in Christ. If they are not believers in Christ's deity, why would they care? Unfortunately, I suspect that hundreds of people are unjustly murdered every day, but no *one* seems to invoke their demise as a cause to condemn an entire lineage of people.

Of course, it is not that it has always been non-Christians who used the unjust death of Jesus as reason to persecute the descendants of Abraham. Far too often, misled Christians were also culpable. As I stated in Chapter 9, to date there has been only one perfect Christian. Hopefully, as we grow in the faith, we become more discerning about the underlying truths of our faith and how those truths should impact our worldview and become less likely to be carried away by influences more temporal than spiritual.

In fact, it was not until the *Nostra Aetate* 5, ratified by the Second Vatican Council on October 28, 1965, that the Catholic Church officially declared itself as not endorsing the doctrine of the responsibility of the Jewish people in the death of Christ. Having said that, let us closely look at the origin of the concept of complicity of the Jewish people in deicide.

Matthew 26:47–27:44 (penned sometime between AD 60 and 65 by Matthew [Levi], a tax collector), Mark 14:1–15:15 (written between AD 55 and 65 by John Mark, not a disciple but "probably knew Jesus personally" according to footnote in the New International Version), and John 18:2–19:24 (authored probably AD 85–90 by John the apostle, son of Zebedee, brother of James) each attest to the Jewish Sanhedrin plotting and carrying out a plan to kill Jesus, while gaining the reluctant cooperation of the Roman government. Each of these authors was Jewish. Luke, of non-Jewish origins (a Gentile Greek) wrote of the same circumstances (about AD 60) in Luke 22:47–23:37. But to find the earliest public accusation, we need to go to the book of Acts (recorded by Luke between A.D. 63 and 70).

"When the day of Pentecost came, they were all together in one place" (Acts 2:1).

"Now there were staying in Jerusalem God-fearing Jews from every nation under heaven" (Acts 2:5, emphasis mine).

169

The Apostle Peter declared, "Fellow *Israelites*, listen to this: Jesus of Nazareth was a man accredited by God to you by miracles, wonders and signs, which God did among you through him, as you yourselves know. This man was handed over to you by God's deliberate plan and foreknowledge; *and you, with the help of wicked men*, put him to death by nailing him to the cross" (Acts 2:22–23, emphasis mine).

"'Therefore, let *all Israel* be assured of this: God has made this Jesus, whom you crucified, both Lord and Messiah.' When the people heard this, they were cut to the heart and said to Peter and the other apostles, 'Brothers, what shall we do?'" (Acts 2:36–37, emphasis mine).

"Those who accepted his message were baptized, and about three thousand were added to their number that day" (Acts 2:41).

From these passages we can deduce several things. The Jews at large were first publicly accused of deicide fifty-one days after Jesus was crucified, and that verbal indictment came from a Jew. According to the footnotes in the New International Version of the Bible, the Romans are inferred in the term "wicked men," which is also translated "those not having the law (that is, Gentiles)." The message was widely accepted as being valid by the Jews present. Taken as a whole, it seems that the Jews were indeed directly responsible for the death of Jesus. However, once we probe beyond this superficial interpretation, we come to a much more startling answer to the question of who is ultimately to blame for this heinous act.

Once more I call your attention to the book of Genesis. In chapter 3 we read an account of the derivation of *original sin* (a term I learned in my first year in parochial school) or the earliest manifestation of man's inherent sin nature. The first few verses have to do with the devil in the form of a serpent tempting Eve and, through her, Adam. The object of the temptation is a certain tree in the garden of Eden that yields fruit of the knowledge of good and evil. In verse 6 we read, "When the woman saw that the fruit of the tree was good for food and pleasing to the eye, and also desirable for gaining wisdom, she took some and ate it. She also gave some to her husband, who was with her, and he ate it."

Now some of you will argue that this story must be taken literally and others that it is best interpreted allegorically. For the purposes of this exercise, I think the important thing to take away is that from the time that mankind came to a point of being able to distinguish good from evil, right from wrong, God's will from man's own, and chose in such a way as to oppose that good, right, and godly will, there was a seemingly insurmountable barrier set up between man and God (if you don't understand this, then I suggest you reread Chapter 8 in my book). At that instant, a bill became due that would have to be paid in full prior to man having any hope of everlasting communion with God. And God, knowing this even before it happened, mentions the solution in Genesis 3:15: "And I will put enmity between you [the serpent/ devil] and the woman, and between your offspring and hers; he [the redeemer/Christ] will crush your head, and you will strike his heel."

This is the first prophecy attesting to the need of someone to ransom those who were in debt, the Messiah. There are many more Old Testament prophecies dealing with this: birth in Bethlehem, being born to a virgin, being a prophet, entering Jerusalem in triumph, being rejected by His own people (the Jews), being betrayed by one of His followers, being tried and condemned and silent before His accusers, being struck and spat on by His enemies, dying by crucifixion in the company of criminals, being given vinegar and gall, others casting lots for His clothing, His bones not being broken, His being raised from the dead, and His current position at God's right hand. But for us to best understand the nature of the causation and blame for Jesus' death, we should focus on the writings of Isaiah, especially the prophecy in chapter 53.

"But he was pierced for *our* transgressions, he was crushed for *our* iniquities; the punishment that brought us peace was on him, and by his wounds *we* are healed" (v. 5, emphasis mine).

"*We* all, like sheep, have gone astray, *each of us* has turned to our own way; and the LORD has laid on him the iniquity of us all" (v. 6, emphasis mine).

"By oppression and judgment he was taken away. Yet who of his generation protested? For he was cut off from the land of the living; for the transgression of *my people* he was punished" (v. 8, emphasis mine).

"Yet it was the LORD'S will to crush him and cause him to suffer, and though the LORD makes his life an offering for sin, he will see *his offspring* and prolong his days, and the will of the LORD will prosper in his hand" (v. 10, emphasis mine).

"After he has suffered, he will see the light of life and be satisfied; by his knowledge my righteous servant will justify *many*, and he will bear *their iniquities*" (v. 11, emphasis mine).

"Therefore I will give him a portion among the great, and he will divide the spoils with the strong, because he poured out his life unto death, and was numbered with the transgressors. For he bore the sin of *many*, and made intercession for the *transgressors*" (v. 12, emphasis mine).

Jesus Himself was fully aware of His purpose and destiny in becoming incarnate. For the purposes of brevity, I will cite only a few verses from the Gospel of Matthew to make my point.

"When they came together in Galilee, he said to them, 'The Son of Man is going to be delivered into the hands of men. They will kill him, and on the third day he will be raised to life'" (17:22–23).

"We are going up to Jerusalem, and the Son of Man will be delivered over to the chief priests and the teachers of the law. They will condemn him to death and will hand him over to the Gentiles to be mocked and flogged and crucified. On the third day he will be raised to life!" (20:18–19).

"As you know, the Passover is two days away—and the Son of Man will be handed over to be crucified" (26:2).

These passages attest to Jesus knowing what lay ahead, and this final quotation from Matthew is a summation of His purpose in letting it happen:

"Then he took a cup, and when he had given thanks, he gave it to them, saying, 'Drink from it, all of you. This is my blood of the covenant, which is poured out *for many for the forgiveness of sins*'" (26:27–28, emphasis mine).

As evidence that the Church fathers grasped the truth of who was actually to blame for Jesus having to die as He did, I will call on a final scriptural witness. This attester hails from a letter written to Hebrew Christians probably before A.D. 70, possibly by Paul, Luke, Barnabas, Apollos, or another author:

"But we do see Jesus, who was made lower than the angels for a little while, now crowned with glory and honor because he suffered death, so that by the grace of God he might taste death *for everyone"* (Hebrews 2:9, emphasis mine).

So, who is it that is ultimately responsible for the death of Jesus? To assign the blame solely to the Jews is tantamount to blaming the hammer that drove the nails through His flesh to affix him to the cross. To find the guilty party, we must examine the fingerprints on the handle of the hammer. When we do, we find that his name is Adam, and her name is Eve, and his name is Noah, and his name is Abraham, and her name is Sarah, and his name is Moses, and David, and Goliath, and Isaiah, and Nebuchadnezzar, and Ruth, and Alexander and Natasha, and Kim, and Adolf, and Mary, and Ahmed, and Juanita, and Sven, and so on. He is white, she is black, he is yellow, she is tan, he speaks French, she speaks Arabic, he is Catholic, she is Protestant, he is young, and she is old.

The number of guilty human parties is limited only to the number of people that lived long enough to break even one of God's commands in deed or even in thought (see Matthew 5:27–28). If there is a group of people we can label "more guilty," then the first name that comes to mind is Greg. Why? Who would you think is more at fault for breaking the speed limit, the person driving a new road who did not notice or perhaps saw but did not believe the regulatory sign, or the person who studied the sign and did his best to post it in a conspicuous place and then purposefully drove too fast?

Saint Peter believed in Jesus as the Christ, yet publicly denied Him. With the possible exception of the thief on the cross, who had limited opportunity to do otherwise, the rest of us who call ourselves Christian have not lagged far behind. Perhaps it is because we are thus especially aware of our responsibility at placing Jesus on the cross that we know that we owe Him so much more than we could ever hope to give in return. We are reduced to a contrite prayer of thankfulness for His love of us despite our utter unworthiness.

GMT

NOTES

PREFACE

1. "Over the Rainbow" *(from The Wizard of Oz)*, Music by Harold Arlen, Lyrics by E.Y. Harburg. © 1938 (Renewed) Metro- Goldwyn-Mayer Inc., © 1939 (Renewed) EMI Feist Catalog Inc. All Rights Controlled and Administered by EMI Feist Catalog Inc. (Publishing) and Alfred Music (Print). All Rights Reserved.

CHAPTER 1: ETERNITY

1. Kurt Vonnegut Jr. (1922–2007). American novelist, essayist, honorary president of the American Humanist Association. Vonnegut studied mechanical engineering at Carnegie Institute of Technology and the University of Tennessee prior to enlisting in the U.S. Army. He was captured in the Battle of the Bulge and taken prisoner to Dresden. That city was firebombed in February 1945. He survived because the prisoners had been taken to an underground meat locker called *Schlachthof Fünf*, which translated means "Slaughterhouse Five." Wikipedia. en.m.wikipedia.org/wiki/Kurt_Vonnegut#sec-tion_1

2. Kurt Vonnegut Jr., *Slaughterhouse-Five or The Children's Crusade* (New York: Delacorte Press, 1969).

CHAPTER 2: HISTORICAL PERSPECTIVES ON HEAVEN

1. Most nonbiblical quotes found at the beginnings of the chapters are from Brainy Quote,
   http://www.brainyquote.com/quotes

2. "Religions of the World Ranked by Number of Adherents."
   http://www.adherents.com/ReligionsByAdherents.html/

3. "History of atheism." Wikipedia.
   http://en.wikipedia.org/wiki/History

4. Op. cit. Number obtained by adding the estimated number of those estimated for Hinduism (900 million) to those estimated for Buddhism (376 million).

5. "Theory of everything"
   Wikipedia.en.m.wikipedia.org/wiki/Theory-of-everything

6. "The Buddhist Concept of Heaven and Hell."
   http://www.viet.net/anson/ebud/whatbudbelieve/303.html

7. Baron Friedrich von Hugel, *Eternal life: A Study of Its Implications and Applications (Edinburgh,* U.K.: T&T Clark, 1929).

8. "Biblical Apologetics 4," BibleMaster.com.
   http://www.biblemaster.com/studies/study.asp?study_id=1268

9. Alden Bass, "The Ancient Origins of Hinduism," Apologetics Press.

http://www.apologeticspress.org/apcontent.aspx?
category=8&article=1408

10 "The Vedas," Internet Sacred Text Archive. "The Vedas are the primary texts of Hinduism…Scholars have determined that the Rig Veda, the oldest of the four Vedas, was composed about 1500 B.C. and codified about 600 B.C. It…was finally committed to writing… at some point after 300 B.C. The Vedas contain hymns, incantations, and rituals from ancient India."
http://www.sacredtests.com/hin/index.htm

11. *The Compact Guide to World Religions,* Dean C. Halverson, ed. (Minneapolis: Bethany House Publishers, 1996) p. 88.

12 Ibid.

13. Andrew Powell, *Living Buddhism* (New York: Harmony Books, 1989).

14. Malcolm David Eckel, "Buddhism," *World Religions the Illustrated Guide,* Michael D. Coogan, ed. (London: Duncan Baird Publishers, 1998).

15. *The Compact Guide to World Religions, Dean C.* Halverson, ed. (Minneapolis: Bethany House, 1996) p. 55.

16. Ibid. p. 59.

17. "Rebirth (Buddhism)."
en.m.wikipedia.org/wiki/Rebirth_(Buddhism)

18. "Nirvana." Overview. Wikipedia.
http://en.wikipedia.org/wiki/Nirvana

19. "Life and Death—Hinduism."
death.findyourfate.com/life-after-death/hinduism.html

20. "Religion in Mesopotamia." Wikipedia.
http://en.wikipedia.org/wiki/Religion in Mesopotamia

21. "List of Roman deities." Wikipedia. "A lectisternium is a banquet for the gods, at which they appear as images seated on couches, as if present and participating. In describing the lectisternium of the Twelve Great Gods in 217 BC, the Augustan historian Livy places the deities in gender-balanced pairs: Jupiter- Juno, Neptune-Minerva, Mars-Venus, Apollo-Diana, Vulcan- Vesta, Mercury-Ceres." pedia.org/wiki/List_of_Roman_deities

22. Ibid. "Mesopotamian religion was polytheistic, worshipping over 2000 different deities."

23. "The Spectrum of Religions and Religious Beliefs." *The Compact Guide to World Religions,* Dean C. Halverson, ed. (Minneapolis: Bethany House, 1996).

24. "Religions of the World ranked by Number of Adherents" Number estimated by adding "primal-indigenous" (300 million) and African traditional & Diasporic (100 million). http://www.adherents.com/ReligionsByAdherents. html/

25. "Death, Burial, and the Afterlife in Greece and Rome." places.com/evidence-of-the-afterlife-in-greece-and-rome. htm

26. "The Great Unknown—Some Views of the Afterlife." ThinkQuest.library.thinkquest.org/16665/afterliferome.htm

27. "Caligula 'thought he was a god.'" BBC News, August 8, 2003.
http://news.bbc.co.uk/2/hi/europe/3135821.stm

28. *The Compact Guide to World Religions,* Dean C. Halverson, ed. (Minneapolis: Bethany House, 1996) p. 15.

29. "Biblical Apologetics 4. Genesis 1:1-1." BibleMaster.
http://www.biblemaster.com/studies/study.asp?Study_id=1268

30. Religions A–Z" Zoroastrianism.
http://www.religionfacts.com/zoroastrianism/index.htm

31. "Religions of the World ranked by Number of Adherents."
http://www.adherents.com/Religions   ByAdherents.html/

32. Friedrich Wilhelm Nietzsche (1844–1900). "German philosopher, poet, composer, cultural critic, and classical philologist." Probably best known for his thesis statement "God is dead," which appears several times in his writing. He developed the concept of the Übermensch ("superman,"

"overman") in his manuscript *Thus Spoke Zarathustra*.
"Zarathustra's gift of the overman is given to mankind…
Zarathustra presents the overman as the creator of new values,
and he appears as a solution to the problem of the death of
God and nihilism." "The overman does not follow morality
of common people…but instead rises above the notion of
good and evil and above the herd." **en.m.wikipedia.org/
wiki/Friedrich_Nietzsche#section_2**

33. "Life After Death —And the Nature of Heaven and
Hell." Hindu Website. **http://www.hinduwebsite.com/
Zoroastrianism/afterlife.asp**

34. "Life After Death—Zoroastrianism."
**http://death.findvourfate.com/life-after-death/
zoroastrianism.html**

35. "Paradise: Zoroastrianism." Heaven and Hell, According to
Various Religions.
**http://www.neatorama.com/2007/03/23/heaven-and-
hell-according-to-various-religions/**

36. "Religions of the World Ranked by Number of Adherents."
**http://www.adherents.com/ReligionsByAdherents.
html/**

37. "The Origins of Taoism."
**http://www.bbc.co.uk/religion/religions/taoism/
history/ history.shtml**

38. *The Compact Guide to World Religions,* Dean C. Halverson,
ed. (Minneapolis: Bethany House, 1996) p. 217.

39. Julia Hardy, "Taoism Beliefs, Taoism Afterlife and Salvation." **http://www.natheos.com/Library/Taoism/Beliefs/Afterlife- andSalvation.html**

40. "The Afterlife," Personal Tao. **http://personaltao.com/taoismlibrary/articles/the-afterlife/**

41. Op. cit.

42. Op. cit.

43. Mitchell G. Bard. "Pharisees, Sadducees, and Essenes," Jewish Virtual Library. **http://www.jewishvirtuallibrary.org/jsource/History/sadducees_pharisees_essens.html**

44. Judaism 101. "Olam Ha-Ba: The Afterlife." **http://www.jewfaq.org/olamhaba.htm**

45. Ibid.

46. Religion Facts. "Jewish Beliefs on the Afterlife." **facts.com/Judaism/beliefs/afterlife.htm**

47. "The belief of 'Heaven' in Islam." **HilalPlaza.com. http://www.hilalplaza.com/islam/Heaven. html**

48. **"Qur'an & Hadith." Alim Surah 37 As-Saffat vs. 45– www.alim.org/library/quran/surah/english/37/MAL**

49. "The belief of 'Heaven' in Islam." HilalPlaza.com. http://**www.hilalplaza.com/islam/Heaven.html**

50. "How many prophets are there in Islam?" Yahoo Answers **https://answers.yahoo.com/question/index?qid=20061117020116AAx1Pyf**

51. "Muslims have been taught that the early texts of the Bible were corrupted by the Jews and the Christians. This is known as the doctrine of *tahrif*, or alteration." *The Compact Guide to World Religions*, Dean C. Halverson, ed. (Minneapolis: Bethany House, 1996) p. 111.

52. "The degrees and levels of Paradise and Hell, and the deeds that take one to them." Islam Question and Answer. **http://islamqa.info/en/ref/27075**

53. It was reported in the hadeeth of al-Miqdaam ibn Ma'di Karb that the Prophet (salAllahu alaihi wasalam) said: "Islam the Way of Life: The six blessings of the martyrs." **http://sharingknowledgeofislam.blogspot.com/2011/05/six-blessingsof-martyrs.html**

54. Quaranic verses having to do with Houris: Quaran 52:17–19: "They will recline on thrones arranged in ranks. And we shall marry them or Huris with wide lovely eyes." Quaran: 37:40–48: "They will sit with bashful, dark-eyed virgins, as chaste as the sheltered eggs of ostriches." Quran 44: 51–55: "Yes and we shall wed them to dark eyed houri." See also Quaran 55:56–57, Quaran 55:72, Quaran 78:31, Quaran 78:33–34, Quaran 56:7–40, and others. Syed Kam- ran Mirza, "Islamic Heaven."

55. "Houri." New World Encyclopedia. pedia.org/entry/ Houri

56. "An-Naba (The Announcement) (78:33)" Compare Translations. Quran360. **http://web.quran360.com/site/ compare/tr/59/ch/78/v/33**

57. "Chapter 44 surat l-dakhan [The Smoke] vs. 54." Quaranic ArabicCorpus. Corpus.quran.com/

58. "Each time we sleep with a Houri we find her a virgin." Al-ItqanfiUlum al-Qur'an, p. 351.

59. Maxfield Parrish (1870–1966). American painter and illustrator.

60. "Besides, the penis of the Elected never softens. The erection is eternal." Al-Itqan fiUlum al-Qur'an, p. 351.

61. "Every man who enters paradise shall be given 72 (seventy-two) houris; no matter at what age he had died, when he is admitted into paradise, he will become a thirty-year-old, and shall not age any further. A man in paradise shall be given virility equal to that of one hundred men." TIRMZI, vol. 2, page 138. **muhammad-ummah.blogspot.com/2012/08/ tirmzi-vol.html**

62. Al Ghazzali, Ihya Uloom Ed-Din. The Revival of the Religious Sciences, vol. 4. **http://www.nderf.org/Islamic_ views_death.htm**

63. Only 20 percent of Muslims live in the Middle East and North Africa while another 62 percent live in Asia-Pacific locales. Muslim World. Wikipedia. en.m.wikipedia.org/wiki/Muslim_ world

64. "Misconceptions Regarding Hoor." **http://islamicreplies.ucoz.com/2/Misconceptions_ Regarding_ Hoor.html**

65. "72 Virgins." Wikiislam. **http://wikiislam.net/wiki/72_Virgins**

66. Adolph (later Arthur) "Harpo" Marx (1888–1964). American comedian.

67. Go *West*, Marx Brothers film produced by Jack Cummings, distributed by MGM, released December 6, 1940.

68. L. Frank Baum, *The Wonderful Wizard of Oz* (New York: Puffin Books, 2008, first published in 1900) See chapter 11, "The Wonderful City of Oz."

69. 69. William-Adolphe Bouguereau (1825–1905). French academic painter.

70. N.T. Wright (1948–). "Retired Anglican bishop and New Testament Scholar. He is currently Research Professor of New Testament and Early Christianity at St. Mary's College, University of St. Andrews in Scotland" *en.wikipedia.org/wiki/N._T._Wright*

71. *N. T. Wright, Surprised by Hope: Rethinking Heaven, the Resurrection, and the Mission of the Churc*h (New York: HarperOne, 2008) pp. 35– 36.

72. Ibid. p. 41.

CHAPTER 3: TIME

1. Alfred North Whitehead. Wikipedia. **http://en.wikipedia.org/wiki/Alfred_North_Whitehead**

2. M.C. Escher's "Drawing Hands" © 2014 The M.C. Escher Company-The Netherlands. All rights reserved. **www. mcescher. com.** Used by permission.

3. Augustine of Hippo. Algerian. "Was bishop of Hippo Regius (present-day Annaba, Algeria)… is generally considered one of the greatest Christian thinkers of all times. His writings were very influential in the development of Western Christianity." Wikipedia. **http://en.m.wikipedia. org/wiki/Augustine_of_Hippo**

4. Isaac Newton (1642–1727). English physicist, mathematician, astronomer, natural philosopher, alchemist, and theologian.

5. Albert Einstein (1879–1955). German theoretical physicist. 1921 Nobel laureate in physics.

6. "Time dilation." Wikipedia. **en.wikipedia.org/wiki/time dilation**

7. "How Black Holes Work." How Stuff Works.

science.howstuffworks.com/dictionary/astronomy-terms/ black-hole1.htm

8. "Schwarzschild's Spacetime: Introducing the Black Hole." Physics.syr.edu/courses/modules/lightcone/schwarzchild. html.

9. "Ann E. Ewing Dies," The Washington Post, Sunday, August 1, 2010. http://www.washingtonpost.com/wp-dyn/content/article/2010/07/31/AR2010073102772.html

10. "Black Holes." National Earth Science Teachers Association. http://www.windows2universe.org/theuniverse/BH.html

11. "Alan Guth, MIT Department of Physics." web.mit.edu/physics/people/faculty/guth_alan.html

12. "Inflation (cosmology)." Wikipedia. en.m.wikipedia.org/wiki/Inflation_(cosmology)

13. "What's 96 Percent of the Universe Made Of? Astronomers Don't Know". Space.com Article by Clara Moskowitz, published on May 12, 2011

CHAPTER 4: COSMOLOGY: THE NECESSITY OF A NEW HEAVEN AND NEW EARTH

1. "Age of the Earth—Key Topics on Geology." Wikipedia. en.m.wikipedia.org/wikipedia.org/wiki/Age_of_the_Earth

2. Adam Frank "The Sun's Death: Sooner Rather than Later?" McGraw- Hill Education, 2001. **http://www.mhhe.com/physsci/astronomy/uspeak/ sept_00_ uspeak.mhtml**

3. "Future of the Earth." Wikipedia. "The luminosity of the Sun will steadily increase, resulting in a rise in the solar radiation reaching the Earth. This will cause a decrease in the level of carbon dioxide in the atmosphere." **http:// en.wikipedia.org/wiki/Future_of_the_Earth**

4. Ibid. "The long-term trend is for plant life to die off altogether. The resulting loss of oxygen replenishment will cause the extinction of animal life a few million years later."

5. Ibid. "The atmosphere will become a 'moist greenhouse' leading to a runaway evaporation of the oceans … stratosphere would contain increasing levels of water … broken down by photo dissociation by ultraviolet radiation, allowing hydrogen to escape the atmosphere … a loss of the world's sea water by about 1.1 billion years from the present."

6. John H. Debes and Marc J. Kuchner, "Dead Stars and Doomed Planets," *Astronomy,* March 2012.

7. Op. cit. "It is likely to expand to swallow both Mercury and Venus, reaching a maximum radius of 1.2 astronomical units." (The current distance from the earth to the sun is considered 1.0 astronomical unit.)

8. "Helium flash." Wikipedia. "The explosive nature of the helium flash arises…once temperatures reach 100 million–200 million Kelvins (about 180–360 million degrees Fahrenheit) and helium fusion begins…the temperature rapidly increases… further increasing the fusion rate…. This runaway reaction quickly climbs to about 100 billion times the star's normal energy production." **http://enwikipedia.org/w/index.php? title=Helium_flash&oldid=510609942**

9. "White Dwarf Stars." NASA's Imagine the Universe! "An Earth-sized white dwarf has a density of 1 x 109 kg/m3 … 200,000 times as dense [as the earth]." **Imagine.gsfc.nasa. gov/docs/science/know_12/dwarfs.html**

10. "Stellar Evolution: White Dwarfs." "After a billion years the typical white dwarf is down to 0.001 the luminosity of the Sun." http://abyss.uoregon.edu/~js/ast122/lectures/lec17. html

11. "Future of the Earth." Wikipedia. "The drag from the Solar atmosphere may cause the orbit of the Moon to decay…the orbit… will cross the Earth's Roche Limit. Tidal interaction with the Earth would then break apart the moon, turning it into a ring system." **http://en.wikipedia.org/wiki/Future_of_the_Earth**

12. Ron Cowen, "Andromeda on Collision Course with the Milky Way," Nature, May 31, 2012. **http://www.nature.com/news/andromeda-oncollision- course-with-the-milky-way-1.10765**

13. "Kuiper Belt & Oort Cloud," Solar System Exploration, NASA. "In1950, Dutch astronomer Jan Oort proposed that certain comets come from a vast, extremely distant, spherical shell of icy bodies surrounding the solar system… now named the Oort Cloud…a distance of 5,000–100,000 astronomical units." **http:// solarsystem. nasa. gov/ planets/ profile. cfm? Object=KBOs&Display=Overview Long**

14. John H. Debes and Marc J. Kuchner, "Dead Stars and Doomed Planets," *Astronomy*, March 2012.

15. Michael Carroll, "Tour our Wet Solar System," *Astronomy*, July 2012. "Saturn's rings contain 26 million times as much water as all of Earth's oceans combined.… If the surface ice is between 6 and 18.5 miles …thick, then Europa's liquid ocean would be approximately 60 miles deep and hold twice the water contained in all of Earth's oceans."

16. Klaus Schmidt International Space Fellowship, "Astronomy Question of the Week: How long will the Sun continue to shine?" **fellowship.com;news/art9727/astronomy-question-of-the- week-how-long-will-the-sun-continue-to-shine**

17. "Red Dwarf." Wikipedia. "A red dwarf with 0.1 solar mass may continue burning for 10 trillion years." **http://en.wikipedia.org/wikiRed_dwarf**

18. Edwin Powell Hubble (1889–1953). American astronomer, pioneer in the field of extra-galactic astronomy, published research implicating shift in light spectrum ("red shift") as a

correlate to speed, and, therefore, distance of other galaxies' recession from our own Milky Way. He helped prove that the universe is expanding.

19. "Distant Galaxies Confirm Accelerating Growth of Universe."**www.space.com/15247-universe-acceleration-dark-energyquasars.html**

20. 20."Chronology of the Universe." Wikipedia. **http://en.wikipedia.org/wiki/Chronology_of_the_ universe**

21. Ibid.

22. Ibid.

23. "Shoemaker-Levy 9/Jupiter Impact." **www.solarviews.com/eng/impact.htm**

24. Oliver Hardy, born Norvell Hardy (1892–1955). American actor whose film career spanned both silent and sound-capable films. One-half of the comedy team of Laurel and Hardy. **http://en.m.wikipedia.org/wiki/Oliver_ Hardy#section_2**

25. Stan Laurel, born Arthur Stanley Jefferson (1890–1965). English comic actor, writer, film director famous as the first half of the comedy team Laurel and Hardy. http:// en.m.wikipedia. org/wiki/Stan_Laurel

CHAPTER 5: SEX

1. "Hedonism." Wikipedia. "Hedonism is a school of thought that argues that pleasure is the only intrinsic good. In very simple terms, a hedonist strives to maximize net pleasure (pleasure minus pain).... Democritus seems to be the earliest philosopher on record to have categorically embraced a hedonistic philosophy."
   http://en.m.wikipedia.org/wiki/Hedonism#section_2

2. "So, God created mankind in his own image, in the image of God he created them; male and female he created them" (Genesis 1:27).

3. "That is why a man leaves his father and mother and is united to his wife, and they become one flesh" (Genesis 2:24).

4. The majority of the factual information on neuroanatomy and biochemistry cited here is from "Neuroanatomy and Physiology of the 'Brain Reward System' in Substance Abuse." **orado.edu/cadd/a_drug/essays/essay4.htm**

CHAPTER 6: SPECIAL ABILITIES AND SENSATIONAL SENSES

1. John Gillespie Magee Jr. (1922–1941). American who flew for the Royal Canadian Air Force. Born in Shanghai, China, to an American father and a British mother who were Anglican missionaries. He joined the Canadian Air Force prior to the United States entering World War II. He was killed in a mid-air collision over Lincolnshire, England, and was age 19 at the time of his death.

2. "Light." Wikipedia.
   http://en.m.wikipedia.org/wiki/Visible_light

3. "Glossary of Terms."
   **http://www.astro.virginia.edu/~jh8h/astr124/glossary.
   html**

4. "The Cosmic Microwave Background."
   www.astro.ubc.ca/people/scott/cmb_intro.html

5. "Amazing Animal Senses," Neuroscience for Kids.
   http://faculty.washington.edu/chudler/amaze.html

6. "Air Pressure and Altitude above Sea Level." The Engineering
   ToolBox.
   **http://www.engineeringtoolbox.com/air-
   altitudepressured_462.html**

7. "What will be the air temperature at the altitude of
   14,000 feet above central Saudi Arabian land?" Yahoo!
   Answers. "The average lapse rate, according to the Standard
   Atmosphere is 0.65 C per 100 meters."
   **http://in.answers.yahoo.com/question/index?
   qid=20090319052433AASg.J2T**

8. "How much detail could the Hubble telescope see?" Ask
   MetaFilter.
   **ask.metafilter.com/121958/How-much-could-the-
   Hubble- telescope-see**

9. "Speed of Sound in Some Common Solids." The Engineering
   ToolBox.

www.engineeringtoolbox.com/sound-speed-solidsd_713. html

10. Ibid.

11. Ibid.

12. "Hearing range." **Wikipedia. en.m.wikipedia.org/wiki/Hearing_range**

13. "How Do Dolphins Hear?" **Dolphins-World.com.phinsworld.com/how_do_ dolphins_ hear.html**

14. "Understanding a Dog's Senses." Dog Breed Info Center. **http://www.dogbreedinfo.com/articles/dogsenses.htm**

15. Amazing Animal Senses," Neuroscience for Kids. **ington.edu/chudler/amaze.html**

16. Ibid.

17. Ibid.

18. *Grand Canyon Suite.* Composed between 1929 and 1931, by Ferde Grofé (1892–1972), American composer, arranger and pianist. Grofé arranged George Gershwin's *Rhapsody in Blue.*

CHAPTER7 : DISCOVERING THE UNIVERSAL TRUTHS

1. Claudius Ptolemy (AD 90–168). Greek mathematician, astronomer, geographer, astrologer. **en.m.wikipedia.org/wiki/Ptolemy**

2. Leonardo da Vinci (1452–1519). Italian Renaissance artist, painter, sculptor, architect, musician, scientist, mathematician, engineer, inventor, anatomist, geologist, cartographer, botanist, writer. **http://wikipedia.org/wiki/ Leonardo_da_Vinci**. As I remember hearing, he could bend a horseshoe using only his bare hands so that the heels of the shoe faced opposite directions.

3. Isaac Newton (1642–1727). "English natural philosopher, generally regarded as the most original and influential theorist in the history of science. In addition to his invention of the infinitesimal calculus and a new theory of light and color, Newton transformed the structure of physical science with his three laws of motion and the law of universal gravitation." Robert A. Hatch, "Sir Isaac Newton." **web.clas.ufl.edu/users/ufhatch/pages/01-courses/ current- courses/08srnewton.htm**

4. Albert Einstein (1879–1955). German-born theoretical physicist and 1921 Nobel laureate in physics. Discoverer of the photoelectric effect and helped establish quantum theory. Author of the theories of general relativity (the geometric theory of gravitation published in 1916) and special relativity (the theory of measurement in an inertial frame of reference published in 1905). en.m.wikipedia.org/ wiki/Special_relativity

5. Plato (c. 428–347 BC). Classical Greek philosopher, mathematician, student of Socrates and mentor to Aristotle. Helped lay the foundation of Western philosophy and science. **en.m.wikipedia.org/wiki/Plato**

6. Plato's *The Republic* was probably written around 380 BC. "Plato's best-known work concerns the definition of justice and the order and character of the just city-state and the just man." **en.m.wikipedia.org/wiki/Plato**

7. "The philosopher is the man who loves (Greek *philein*) wisdom (*sophia*) in the widest sense, including especially learning, knowledge and truth." Desmond Lee, *Plato, The Republic*, (New York: Penguin Books, 1955) p. 192.

8. 8. Ibid., p. 194.

9. "Superstrings," NASA's Imagine the Universe, July 5, 2005. **http://imagine.gsfc.nasa.gov/docs/science/mysteries_l2/superstring.html**

10. "The essential idea behind string theory is this: all of the different 'fundamental' particles of the Standard Model are really just different manifestations of one basic object: a string…can oscillate in different ways…if it oscillates in a certain way…we see an electron. But if it oscillates some other way…we call it a photon, or a quark…" "What is String Theory?" **www.nuclecu. unam.mx/-~alberto/physics/string.html.** This gives me cause to wonder. Matter, from galaxies, down to atoms, seems to manifest the property termed "spin." Oscillations of different frequencies code for different fundamental particles. It seems to me that strings

may also possess something analogous to spin inherently in their nature. If so, what does the orientation of that "spin" for a string at a given frequency code for? Could this be what differentiates matter from dark matter? My hunch is that it might code for something even more basic but less understood: dimensionality itself.

11. "Superstring theory." This is a version of string theory that incorporates fermions (energy manifest as matter), bosons (energy manifest as a force carrier like gravity) and supersymmetry (see below). Wikipedia. **en.m.wikipedia. org/wiki/Superstring_ theory**

12. "String theories are classified according to whether or not the strings are required to be closed loops, and whether or not theparticle spectrum include fermions. In order to include fermions in string theory, there must be a special kind of symmetry called supersymmetry, which means for every boson there is a corresponding fermion. So supersymmetry relates the particles that transmit force to the particles that make up matter." The Official String Theory Website. **www. superstringtheory.com/basics/basic4.html**

13. Max Karl Ernst Ludwig Planck (1858–1947). German theoretical physicist. "Was able to deduce the relationship between the energy and the frequency of radiation.... In a paper published in 1900, he announced his derivation of the relationship: this was based on the revolutionary idea that the energy emitted by a resonator could only take on discrete values or quanta. The energy for a resonator of frequency v is hv where h is a universal constant, now called Planck's constant. Nobel Prize in Physics 1918." Nobelprize.

org. **www.nobelprizes/ physics/laureates/1918/planck-bio.html**

14. James Clerk Maxwell (1831–1879). English. He postulated the theory of electromagnetism. Quotation: "We have strong reason to conclude that light itself—including radiant heat and other radiation, if any—is an electromagnetic disturbance in the form of waves propagated through the electro-magnetic field according to electro-magnetic laws." "Who Was James Clerk Maxwell?" **www.clerkmaxwellFoundation.org/html/who_was_Maxwell_html**

15. Michael Faraday (1791–1867). British. "Received little formal education…the best experimentalist in the history of science … established that magnetism could affect rays of light and that there was an underlying relationship between the two phenomena." Wikipedia. **en.m.wikipedia.org/wiki/Michael Faraday**

16. "Weak interaction." Wikipedia. **http://en.m.wikipedia.org/wiki/Weak_interaction**

17 "The Strong Nuclear Force." **http://aether.lbl.gov/elements/stellar/strong/strong.html**

18. "Questions and Answers about the Origin of Inertia and the Zero-Point Field." **www.calphysics.org/questions.html**

19. 19.   Rodney D. Holder "Is the Universe Designed?" FIMA FRAS Faraday Paper No. 10, Faraday Institute for Science and Religion, St. Edmund's College, Cambridge, U.K. Holder was formerly a priest and carried out post-doctoral research in astrophysics at Oxford. Holder is the author of *God, the Multiverse, and Everything.*

20. "Savant syndrome." Wikipedia.
    http://en.wikipedia.org/wiki/Savant_syndrome

21. "Moron (psychology)." Wikipedia. "Idiot" (IQ of 0–25), "imbecile" (IQ of 26–50), "moron" (IQ of 51–70).
    http://en.m.wikipedia.org/wiki/M or on (psychology) #section_1

22. D. A. Treffert. "The savant syndrome: an extraordinary condition. Asynopsis: past, present, future." *Philosophical transactions of the Royal Society B: Biological Sciences* 364 (1522): 1351–1357.

23. "The Lemke-Leslie Miracle."
    http://www.fairybookshelf.com/cms/index.php?
    option=com_content&view=article&id=322:thelemkel esliemiracle&catid=40:exem-true-stories&Itemid=75

24. "Piano Concerto #1," composed between November 1874 and February 1875, revised in 1879 and again in 1888. http://www.wikipedia.org/wiki/Piano_Concerto_No_1_ **(Tchaikovsky)**

25. Pyotr Ilyich Tchaikovsky (1840–1893). Russian composer of concert and theatrical music. Was the guest conductor at

the inaugural concert at Carnegie Hall in New York City in 1891.
http://www.wikipedia.org/wiki/Pyotr_Ilyich_ Tchaikovsky #section_1

26. Rain Man. 1988 movie featuring Dustin Hoffman, Tom Cruise, and Valeria Golino. Directed by Barry Levinson. IMDb http://m.imdb.com/title/tt0095953/

27. Dustin Hoffman (1937–). American television, stage and film actor whose acting career spans from 1960 to present. Two-time Academy Award winner and recipient of AFI Life Achievement Award. **http://en.m.wikipedia.org/wiki/ Dustin_Hoffman**

28. "10 Most Fascinating Savants in the World." Neatorama. **http://www.neatorama.com/2008/09/05/10-most-fascinating-savantsin-the-world/**

29. "Kim Peek." Wikipedia. http://en.wikipedia.org/wiki/Kim_Peek.

30. "Daniel Tammet: Brainman" 10 Most Fascinating Savants in the World. Neatorama. **http://www.neatorama. com/2008/09/05/10-mostfascinatingsavants-in-the-world/**

31. Ibid.

CHAPTER 8: MAKING LIGHT OF GOD

1. "World's Largest Neutrino Observatory Built at South Pole." LiveScience. **http://www.livescience.com/9164-worldlargest-neutrinoobservatory-built-south-pole.html**

2. Neutrino Mass: "The current limits from cosmological considerations are less than about 0.05 eV (one millionth of the electron mass!).... The heaviest neutrino must be between about a ten-millionth and a millionth of the electron mass." The mass of an electron is $9.10938188 \times 10^{-31}$ kilograms. To obtain an approximation of the maximum mass, I multiply electron mass in Kg. x 2.2 lb/Kg. x 16 oz./lb. x 1,000,000 $9.1094 \times 2.2 \times 16 \times 1,000,000 = 3.2065 \times 10^{-39}$. **www.phy.Princeton.edu/borexino/nu-mass.html**

3. Superman. Comic-book character created by writer Jerry Siegel and artist Joe Shuster. He first appeared in Action Comics #1 in June 1938. He is armed with multiple superpowers, including super strength, the ability to fly, and x-ray vision that allows him to see through most materials but not lead. Two known vulnerabilities: a substance called Kryptonite and a lady known as Lois Lane. **http://en.m.wikipedia.org/wiki/Superman#section_3**

4. "Supernovas: Making Astronomical History Neutrinos." SNEWS **http://snews.bnl.gov/popsci/neutrino.html**

5. Britney Spears (1981–). American singer, songwriter, dancer, entertainer, recording artist. **http://en.m.wikipedia.org/wiki/Britney_Spears**

6. "Oops! ...I Did It Again." Lyrics by Max Martin and Rami Yacoub. Released in 2000.

7. Charlton Heston (1923–2008). American actor, film director, civil rights and gun rights activist, past president of the National Rifle Association. Born John Charles Carter.

8. Anselm of Canterbury (1033–1109). Roman Catholic Archbishop of Canterbury, England. **http://en.m.wikipedia.org/wiki/Anselm_of_Canterbury**

9. Peter Abelard (1079–1142). French scholastic philosopher, theologian, and logician. **http://en.m.wikipedia.org/wiki/Peter_Abelard**

10. Agatha Christie (1890–1976). British novelist and playwright who penned mostly crime stories but did author some romances under the pseudonym of Mary Westmacott. **http://en.m.wikipedia.org/wiki/Agatha_Christie**

11. C. S. Lewis (1898–1963). Irish-born novelist, poet, academic, medievalist, literary critic, essayist, lay theologian, and Christian apologist. Close friend and co-faculty member at Oxford University with J.R.R. Tolkien. **http://en.m.wikipedia.org/wiki/C._S._Lewis**

CHAPTER 9: RELATIONSHIP AND THE SEARCH FOR SIGNIFICANCE

1. *Star Wars.* A series of five science fiction movies released between 1977 and 2002, created by George Lucas. Third highest grossing film series behind only the Harry Potter and James Bond films.

2. Michelangelo (1475–1564). Italian sculptor, painter, architect, and poet of the Italian Renaissance period. **http://en.m.wikipedia.org/wiki/Michelangelo**

3. A. E. Housman (1859–1936). English classical scholar and poet. **http://en.m.wikipedia.org/wiki/A._E._Housman.**

4. Red Skelton (1913–1997). American entertainer best known for being a national radio and television and film comedian. **http://en.m.wikipedia.org/wiki/Red_Skelton**

www.ingramcontent.com/pod-product-compliance
Lightning Source LLC
Chambersburg PA
CBHW051146120626
46547CB00012B/970